The
RECRUITMENT
ROLLERCOASTER

AVOID THE TIGHT TURNS AND STEEP SLOPES OF STARTING YOUR OWN RECRUITMENT AGENCY

JOSHUA RAYNER

Book design by: SWATT Books Ltd

Printed in the United Kingdom
First Printing, 2021

ISBN: 978-1-7398879-0-2 (Paperback)
ISBN: 978-1-7398879-1-9 (eBook)

Joshua Rayner
Wokingham, Berkshire

Contents

Acknowledgements

I would like to thank the following people, for whom without this book and journey wouldn't have been possible.

First and foremost, thank you to my beautiful wife Zoe for your constant love and support. To my amazing kids, Ruby, Sofia and Harry, who make every long day worthwhile. To my mum – Kim, and my dad – Paul, for a wonderful upbringing, and for affording me the lessons and the strong values that have guided me through life. A huge shoutout to John Sims and Sanjay Gandhi for mentoring me and helping me to pivot when I was gazing in the wrong direction. To Simon King who gave the sagest business advice I have ever received. To Claire Robbin and Sam Pearce for your help with the editing and publishing of this book. Lastly, thank you to Russell Jervis for being the voice of reason, and helping me take the business from 0 – 100.

Foreword

This book is written by Joshua Rayner who I have had the pleasure to mentor one-to-one.

What strikes me about Joshua is his can-do attitude and the will to get things done rather than talk about ideas. He is someone who wants to be one of life's successes. He has achieved so much in such a short period of time, giving him the authority to help others on their journey to success.

This book can only be described as a recipe for success and will give the reader a framework to succeed in business and more importantly in the recruitment industry. This is where Joshua excels and is a now leading authority. His company, Rayner Personnel, has become the number one recruitment company for the UK property sector.

Joshua now spends more of his time mentoring other young entrepreneurs who want to start up their own business and want the shortcuts from somebody who has spent the last fifteen years crafting his and his company's success.

Enjoy this book and be sure to connect with Joshua Rayner – it could be your best-ever business decision.

Sanjay Gandhi
Mentor and Entrepreneur

About the Author

Joshua Rayner lives in Berkshire, England, and is a proud husband and father of three. After a short but notable spell in estate agency and 'smile and dial' telesales, Joshua found his passion for recruitment. Today Joshua is the CEO of Rayner Personnel, the UK's leading recruiter within the property sector. A well-known public speaker and commentator, his opinions on people and property are regularly featured and published within the press.

Born in Leyton Hospital, Whipps Cross, in the mid-1980s, Joshua's family moved to Walthamstow and then Chingford before finally settling in leafy Hertfordshire. Being the eldest of three brothers, the change from the hard-nosed end of the city to a genteel historic county market town profoundly affected the 12-year-old Joshua. He found himself to be the outsider, the alien, the underdog. Being backed into a corner, taken out of his comfort zone for the first time of many, ignitedJoshua's drive to succeed and lead.

Joshua's debut book, *The Recruitment Rollercoaster*, takes the reader on Joshua's journey of discovery, successes, experiences and learnings. With a mission to help others, he offers this book to show you where he made mistakes, and how you can avoid them. Buckle up!

INTRODUCTION

Falling Into Recruitment

Many people tell me that they would like to be in my shoes. They see my success, the nice cars, the suits, the fancy holidays, the vision, and they want a part of it. I can't blame them. I used to look up to others and want the same, and I'd be pretty vocal about it too! It's important to remember, however, that every successful person has taken numerous steps – both up and down the ladder. I begin this book with a blow-by-blow overview of the journey that resulted in the development of my business, Rayner Personnel, and all the grave mistakes I have made along the way.

Beginnings

I was born in Leytonstone, a small town on the Central Line in East London, and until I was twelve years old, we lived five miles from Leytonstone in the Essex town of Chingford. These days it's a gentrified hub, swarming with stylish residents, but when I was young, it was a poor and underprivileged area. My parents decided they wanted to provide me with a better start in life, including better schooling, so at twelve years old, we upped and moved to Bishop's Stortford, an affluent historic market town in Hertfordshire.

This was a far cry from the hubbub of London, although a trip back to the big Smoke was just an hour-long train ride away. Not that it made much difference to me, a twelve-year-old on a bicycle – we may as well have moved to Mars. We made the move during the six-week holiday period, so I didn't have the chance to make many new friends at the beginning. I was lonely in those weeks before school started, and by the time the first day at the local comprehensive rolled around, I was more than ready to make some friends. It was incredibly daunting, not knowing anybody, leaving the family home I'd known for twelve years and starting a new life. Although it was a bit scary, the new chapter became great fun, and I made friends very quickly.

My earliest passion

Before the move, I had already found my passion in life at the age of eight – rugby. I was talented; I knew it, and others knew it. Ultimately, it embodied who I was, and who I believed I would become. Moving to Bishop's Stortford at twelve was when I began to build my first prototype brand of 'Josh'. If there was an elevator pitch for my adolescent self, it would include 'uniquely, maturely talented, and fiercely competitive'. I was the first team rugby captain at my school for both year seven and year eight. Then, in the second year (year eight) of secondary school, I was spotted playing rugby and asked to join another local school. It was well-known for rugby, and the Director of Sport had a spotter come and watch me. As the story goes, the spotter watched me and simply said, "We need this boy in our school!"

So, I gladly took the offer and moved from an average comprehensive to an excellent academic and sporting all-boys school. It was a privilege, and I knew this step would take my rugby career in the right direction. It was different from my old school – startlingly so. It was highly regimented; we had to walk on the right-hand side of the corridors, carry a briefcase, and wear a blazer tied down to the belt buckle. It opened my eyes! I began to excel in this disciplined culture – so much so that I took to it like a military man! I was still a youngster, but I relished preparing all my clothes the night before school. I would eagerly lay out my shirt, pants and socks, and have my shoes shined ready for the following day.

I carried on at the school to sixth form, where I became the first team captain for rugby. Because of my high skill level, I played against students a year or two above me. Rugby became my life, and being captain formed the building blocks for who I am today. At training, I would arrive earlier than the others to set up all the cones and training practises, and would be the last person to leave, keenly storing all the equipment. I consider this time of my life to be where my inner 'Why' came from; that I wanted to help people and show them the way.

Shattered dreams

I assumed that my destiny was mapped out, and that I would continue to take my rugby career further. However, I was about to learn that life doesn't always go as planned. During a normal match, on a normal day, I fell badly and shattered my shoulder. The bones broke into numerous pieces, and in that moment, my hopes for a rugby career were over. I was 18 years old.

From the age of eight, I had performed my biggest passion in life with a true sportsman's devotion. It was only ten years, but back then, that was an entire lifetime. After a decade of commitment, talent and aspiring, I couldn't play anymore. My identity was shattered along with my bones.

I needed four surgical procedures to piece my shoulder back together and was hurled into an untimely existential crisis.

What the hell am I going to do now?

I wasn't very academic. I had been studying business studies and politics just so the head of sixth form could keep an eye on me, and although I was disciplined in sport, academically I was a rebel.

So, where to now? That's when a new avenue opened up for me. I contacted the local recruitment company who I'd done some silver-service waiting for as a school boy and asked them if they knew of any roles where I could use my personality, charm and charisma to build a career. The head partner said "YES" I have just the role working for a local independent estate agent agency. That first "Yes" was where my estate agency rollercoaster journey began, although I didn't realise the consequences of not buckling up before the rollercoaster had started. I soon felt the early twists and turns quite sorely.

Entrepreneurial inklings

Even as a schoolboy I had been driven to make my own way and earn money. I had a paper round at the age of 13, pot washed from 14 and temped for a local recruitment agency from the age of 15 – my first taste of the world of work.

I also took on all kinds of work for this agency, anything to make a bit of money, and this included waitering at events they organised – everything from silver service to running the bar at private functions. It was through this that I learnt the value of creating rapport with people (which earned me some excellent tips!) and the importance of developing good people skills.

A false start

I was 18 years old and ready to go. I was being taken on as a lettings negotiator, which felt very grown up. For my first day at the new job, my mum bought me a nice new suit, watch and pair of shoes – I was fully kitted out and I felt sharp!

I got to drive around in a brand-new Mini Cooper and meet people from all walks of life. I loved the job from the get-go; I enjoyed helping people, I liked the role, and most especially, I relished the lifestyle. Three months into the role, my boss sat me down. He looked serious.

He said, "Josh, we love you. You've got loads of energy and you're doing some deals, but your admin lets you down. It's just not working."

I could feel the blood rush to my face. He was right – I was terrible at spelling and following processes. At that time I was young and naive, and although I wanted to drive around, check properties and rent them out, I didn't enjoy all the follow-up like the admin, tenancy agreements, and proof of identity checks. My boss was sympathetic.

"Look, it's probably our fault, Josh. We need someone more senior, someone who's been there and done it. We should have thought ahead. We wish you well, and we'll give you a glowing reference."

And that was it, as easily as I was in, I was out again.

A real start

Wondering what to do next, I thought about the agency where I had temped and had worked as a waiter. I knew they had a full-time recruitment team and so I picked up the phone and contacted the head partner, John Sims. He confirmed that they wanted to branch out and into the specialist field of property recruitment as well as continuing with their general office, sales, marketing, management, and finance recruitment divisions which they were well known for in the local area and still are today. At that time, at the turn of the millennium, the property market was booming, and John had seen an opportunity!

I said, "I've been working for you since I was 15 years old as a waiter, and now I have experience in estate agency. Why not give me a shot working for you?"

There was a pause.

Then John said, "Hmm. Well, Joshua, you're already a bit of a wild card, as there have been a couple of times that we have called you up and you haven't been available," as I sat with crossed fingers, "but, why not? I'm going to take a punt on you."

The company was in the process of setting up an estate agency desk to cover all things property-driven. I would have a boss above me, Steve McBride, but it would just be the two of us in the division, which meant a high level of autonomy. They offered me a £10,000 basic annual salary, a Yellow Pages, a phone and a dash of training. Over the next two years I learned my craft and Steve and I built the team up to ten people. It was an incredible feeling to be succeeding at such a young age.

Of course, when things are going well, there is often a crossroads, and we hit one – hard! Steve took me aside one day.

"Josh, we're doing so well here, and we're making more revenue just as a division than the rest of the company put together! We should do this on our own. What do you say?"

It didn't take much to tempt me.

I said, "Sure, let's do it!"

Steve called a meeting with John, the owner of the business.

"John, I'm thinking about going. I've had enough. I'm going to set up on my own and I'm taking Josh with me."

A short conversation ensued, and that seemed to be the end of the matter. However, an hour went by and the phone rang. Steve answered, and it was John.

"Steve, why don't you stay? I'll give you some equity in the business. You can call it a different name, so it's got its own identity, and off you go."

After a brief discussion, we decided to accept John's offer. It had proved to be an easy decision for Steve, and now little was going to change for me – I was always going to be Steve's number two. Instead of the excitement of being at the start of our own business, this felt merely like more of the same. I looked up to Steve and learnt so much from him. He cared and was always there to pick me up when I fell down or rightly knock me down a peg if I stepped out of line, but in spite of all that I felt there was something missing. I wanted to steer my own ship - I could feel that drive, I needed to break-free, lead my own team and do things entirely on my own terms.

So, I became more and more disheartened – I so wanted to lead. Without fail, every single week I would say to Steve, "I want your job. One day, I want *your* job."

Another year passed until one day, John and Steve fell out and subsequently Steve announced that he wasn't interested in the company anymore and they had both agreed to liquidate the business. Just like that. At the time, Steve and I had seven employees in Bishop's Gate off Liverpool Street in central London, meaning that it was a fair-sized firm. This was an incredibly unsettling turn of events, particularly being 21 years old and having just bought my first property. The news was announced a day or two before I was due to make my first monthly mortgage payment.

A cheeky proposition

This was a huge turning point for me – I was suddenly redundant! I had to either find a new job or think quickly about an alternative.

But I'm good at this! Why don't I call the liquidators and see if I can buy the business?

I rang them up, without a clue about what to say.

"Look, my boss has made me redundant, and they've liquidated the business. I don't know the process, and I've just bought my first property, I'm 21 years old, I've got £2,000 in my savings account, and I'd like to buy the business."

They knocked me back straightaway – my offer was too low. I realised it had been a long shot, so I set about looking for a new role. Suddenly, out of the blue, just a couple of weeks later, the liquidators called me again.

"Josh, is that deal still available, because we'd like to take you up on your offer"

Bingo!

And with that, I bought the business, along with the database, for £2,000, and I transformed the company into a highly aggressive headhunting recruitment firm.

Young people in new businesses make blunders. I was one of those people. Things were going great in the business until I made a fundamental mistake – I gifted 45% of the business from day one to my number two at the time, Wayne. Wayne was an exceptionally good biller, but I needed to convince him to come into the business with me. To my mind, Wayne was my goldmine, and

I needed his placement revenue from day one to build the business. I couldn't pay him a salary straightaway, but I wanted to incentivise him and give him no possibility to refuse.

After we had set up this arrangement, Wayne and I built the business for another three years. We moved the offices from London to Bishop's Stortford, rebuilt the team, grew again, and everything was going great. That was until Wayne began to lose focus. He went from a top biller – the reason I wanted him on board – to not making any placements at all. Now, he wasn't engaged in the business anymore, and that became a real problem for me. We were in a significant growth stage, and yet it was down to me to generate all the cash. We would pay ourselves each month, but of course with the business share arrangement, I was giving Wayne 45 pence from every single pound taken out! With his now negligible contribution to the business, this just didn't make any sense, financially or professionally. So, I decided to offer to buy Wayne out of the business. I discussed it with him, but he was adamant – he didn't want to go. The only other extreme option was for him to buy me out of the business instead. And so, he did, and I left.

Once again, the rollercoaster had hurtled me towards the ground, so fast this time that I thought I was going to smash into the ground headfirst. Miraculously, that's when I saw the chairlift up ahead.

The next day, I plugged in my computer and set up Rayner Recruitment.

CHAPTER ONE

Twists and Turns – My Business Story

I refer to myself as 'unemployable'. There are many that would agree. This doesn't mean that I am lazy, insufferable or incapable; but I *am* an entrepreneur, and we can be complicated creatures.

How do you know if someone is an entrepreneur? Don't worry – they'll tell you!

I like to do things my way. Over the years, doing things 'my way' has not always produced the best results. Now, with hindsight, I can see where I have faltered.

A difficult decision

It was time to start again. To get going I simply plugged in my PC and went straight to work. Rayner Recruitment was born in my bedroom, I already knew that to be successful in recruitment, you needed to be good at forging good business relationships, and I knew that was something I was exceptional at. I went straight for a client I knew well who I also knew needed my help. This proved to be the case, perhaps too much so, as within a short time they represented 85% of my revenue.

And this is when the first brick wall came into view.

The CEO of this, my largest customer, who as I say is making up a scary 85% of my revenue at this point, invited me to his house for a curry, and asked me to bring all my company books with me, including my invoices and turnover etc. I thought this was a strange request, but nevertheless, I did. This guy was a CEO after all, and I never usually dealt with the CEO. I typically dealt with the HR head or the head of recruitment. This guy was worth about £50million so I didn't know what on earth to expect from sharing a curry in his huge mansion just outside of Cambridge. We sat down.

"Josh, I've got a double-edged sword for you. I know you have just had a child. I know you're good at what you do and thank you so much for the people you have put into our business; you've transformed it and have been a big part of our exponential growth. But we wouldn't be the first property business to decide to have an internal recruitment team. So, we want you to come in and run it for us." Then there was an ominous pause. "But if it's a no, unfortunately you will lose us as a customer."

It was a no-brainer. I couldn't afford to lose his business, as it would cripple me, and so, rather reluctantly, I agreed.

Also, as the CEO had mentioned, as well as changes in my business life, I had taken on all sorts of other responsibilities at a young age. I had bought my first property at the age of 21 and I had recently become a father when just 24. I had met someone, and my beautiful daughter Ruby had entered the world completely bowling me over and fueling my drive to succeed even further to give her the life and opportunities that she deserved. And, with a property to fund and a family to support, the idea of an attractive, stable income was too tempting.

So, I was employed as the internal recruiter for one of the largest property businesses in the UK. We had three locations, in Newcastle, Derby and London, and I put in place all the teams and software for those sites. It was a great experience to spend somebody else's money and to be able to do things differently, because in my own business I'd been working on a shoestring.

For a time, I enjoyed driving around in the nice company car and installing the systems and processes. What I didn't like, however, and I still don't like today (which is probably why I'm unemployable!), was the lack of autonomy. They micromanaged me to within an inch of my life! Sure, there were bonuses – they had bought up my old business and paid up all my invoices, but I still couldn't stand the ball and chain around my neck. I was only six months into the role when I realised that I couldn't stand the environment, yet the contract stated that I was restricted from working in the recruitment industry twelve months after leaving. Upon deciding that I needed to leave, I went down to London to meet the CEO. He was fair.

"Josh, this is my mistake, as well as yours. I should never have boxed-in an entrepreneur. I'm sympathetic, but we've got an agreement, and we need to stick to that agreement. I wish you well in the future, and you never know, one day we might use you again in a different capacity."

The 'agreement' meant that I had to keep away from recruitment for the following twelve months, which was a daunting prospect. Everything I'd done in the years beforehand to build up a brand, a name and reputation in the recruitment industry were null and void for one whole year.

An electric opportunity

It was challenging to decide how I would reinvent myself in the meantime. That was until my best friend at school, Henry, suggested that I could work with him and his dad. Henry's dad had an electrical business that produced converter plugs. These were a revolutionary version of the everyday plug-in adapter in that they changed the voltage to match the device. This gave energy-saving benefits to its users.

Henry said that they wanted a sales director for the business, as they needed someone to get it into high street retailers and build the brand.

They offered me a fantastic six-figure salary and a brand-new Mercedes company car. I was 26 years old. I thought it was an excellent opportunity to work with my best friend, have some fun, and make some good money. I agreed.

During that year, we made multiple trips to Vegas for industry shows, got the product into Homebase, and I made them a million pounds in profit. I enjoyed the job, but once it was getting close to the end of my year-long ban from recruitment, I was getting itchy feet. I decided to have a chat with Henry.

"I love it here, and I've had an amazing year, but I just know that I've got to run my own thing and be the master of my own destiny. You're an entrepreneur who has done so well and that inspires me. I know you will understand that I need to do the same."

Henry regretfully agreed that he understood.

A new approach to recruitment

By now it's August 2012. I set up Rayner Personnel. After running two recruitment companies previously, this time was going to be third time lucky, which subconsciously meant make or break time. This time, it *had* to work, or I was going to give up.

Rayner had been, in its Rayner Recruitment incarnation, a recruitment consultancy focusing on the property industry. This is still quite a broad market, taking in a broad range of property professionals, from administrators, sales and lettings negotiators to property managers and surveyors right up to director level, and every post in-between.

I felt that the estate agency industry was crying out for a new approach to recruitment, and the best way to gain attention and to be seen as a serious player in the sector was to create this sector-specific business specialising in and focusing on attracting and placing skilled property industry professionals in award-winning and leading independent and corporate estate agencies.

This was a fresh approach, built around establishing core, long-lasting relationships where we went the extra mile for both client and candidate.

I also knew headhunting was my strength and that my competitors didn't want to put the effort in to make the 100 outbound calls a day that I was prepared to do. Nor could they deal with the constant rejection from candidates that weren't interested – yet to me, this was like water off a duck's back and all part of the headhunting process. As I saw it, the more headhunting calls and market intelligence gathered, the more interviews were created, and the more placements and revenue were generated.

So, to cover all the needs of the property recruitment sector, I set about creating two separate businesses and brands:

Rayner Personnel: Exec headhunting recruitment for senior calibre candidates within the property sector (3 years+ experience). This focused on the good fee stuff, the higher end recruitment.

Estate Agency All-Stars: A recruitment and training business to support the property industry with a new bloodline. The industry had lost loads of great people due to the 2007/8 credit crisis + an increase in compliance red tape + a squeeze on fees. The industry needed a lifeline of fresh new talent and I wanted to fill that gap! We recruited by advertising across job boards, social media, and at colleges and universities.

Once a candidate applied, we wanted to screen the individual to ensure they had the right behaviours and attitude to make an exceptional estate agent. To do this we developed a unique (at the time) three-stage assessment process:

1) Assess each candidate's CV.
2) Psychometric assessment: we benchmarked the industry and therefore knew what characteristics made up an exceptional estate agent.
3) Win-It-In-a-Minute video: an elevator pitch from each candidate, selling themselves. After all, if they couldn't sell themselves how were they going to sell a service?

We advertised heavily and had around 1,500 applicants per month, and yet would only find 15 people that suited each role. The three-step system meant that even though many applicants had an excellent profile for the job, their video let them down. As a result, it proved to be a good way of sorting the rough from the smooth. After all, in estate agency, being fluent and confident in the way that you present yourself and your proposition is one of *the* key skills required.

The other initiative was that we put every successful candidate through a training course. A young person would come in, perhaps a first jobber, and we'd select them through their CV, video and psychometric profile, and then we would go and find them a job. Once they had secured a position, we put them through a five-day induction course in estate agency. The idea was that, from day one in the job, they'd be six months ahead of those being placed via a local newspaper or just via a job board. This system worked really well, and we received excellent feedback from clients on the quality and knowledge of our placements.

Back in 2013, none of this had ever been done before – to attract, place and train a candidate before they hit the desk running.

Estate agents were used to merely putting a window card with "We are hiring" in their shop window and if they really went to town, they would spend £50 on a job ad in the local paper in the hope that the right candidate would walk past their estate agency or look at the local rag and apply.

Training had always been poor and so I wanted to change that. By providing this training package upfront, each of our placements was able to make a real impact from day one *and* each person felt so much more comfortable in the job from day one.

We were the first recruitment/training provider to ever use video to introduce candidates (even before the iPhone had a selfie camera – I used to ask candidates to purchase a webcam to plug in their desktop/laptop).

Then, in late 2014 we hit a wall; my clients couldn't find enough properties to sell.

"Josh, we love your initiative and we are great supporters of it. Thanks for bringing the candidates, and we love the training before they start, but we've now got no properties to sell. Why would we want a junior sat there on their hands?"

I understood the problem, and so we morphed the estate agent training into an online business. I soon realised, however, that I couldn't get both the Rayner Personnel and the Estate Agency All-Stars revenue going up sufficiently simultaneously, as I was having to split my time and effort equally between the two businesses. As a result, I was only getting 50% results from each and I was finding it exhausting running two businesses simultaneously.

So, in 2016, I decided that enough was enough, and took the tough and necessary decision to sell off Estate Agency All-Stars. I was at burnout trying to run two different businesses, and while they were both making money, it was nothing to write home about. It was lifestyle money – not *proper* money. I decided to sell, move on and put all my efforts into Rayner Personnel.

Three, Two, One... Go!

In 2016 we launched a franchise business with Rayner Personnel. I wanted to grow nationally across the country, and for that I needed a headcount and suitable heads. As luck would have it, I found a great opportunity for a first franchisee'. Sam turned around to me and said, "Josh, I don't want to take the job you've offered me. I want to work with you."

He was in Newbury, and I was in Bishop's Stortford, which would be a massive trek every day. So, instead, we put a basic contract together for a franchise in Newbury, and he generated £300K in year one from a cold start with no recruitment or UK property experience. He absolutely killed it. We were thrilled.

On the back of this first success, we decided to franchise it out further. The concept with franchising was to offer each person who came on board a slice of the pie, working with the Rayner Personnel brand on a self-employed basis as a franchisee. They would each have a dedicated territory for them to provide recruitment services to. The franchise agreement allowed each individual 'to' keep a percentage of the fees each month.

This proved to be an attractive package, and very soon, we had a full set of franchisees, covering most of the UK. However, due to my lack of experience in franchising, in not installing proper processes, procedures, targets and expectations, things didn't quite turn out as I had hoped. Also, each franchise territory was just too large to provide a proper first-class service to each client, and the brand's reputation soon began to suffer as a result. In hindsight, the way we set up the Franchisees just didn't provide the right incentives to improve the situation.

I learned these key lessons about running a network of recruiters:

- To streamline the journeys, for both the client and the candidate
- To provide a head office function to support them
- To appoint a managing director to oversee the onboarding and training of new associates and measure and report PPIs (Personal Performance Indicators)
- To identify where franchisees needed guidance, assistance and support

And I learned some really important lessons for me personally:

1) Make a plan.
2) If you haven't already, make a plan.
3) Make sure you have a plan!

Fast forward to 2020, and we used the period of the Covid-19 pandemic to completely rebuild Rayner Personnel. From having had 13 franchises, in their place we now have a structure of over 25 associates, operating under associate license agreements.

Licensed to thrill

We have pivoted from a franchise model to this licensed model to enable each associate, as a licensee, to operate a smaller area and thus have a viable business. This means that each associate can find better candidates and offer the best service, because they are operating hyper-local, on a clearly defined territory patch, utilising and dedicating their time and their local knowledge to helping people.

As a recruiter, I got it wrong with my strategy for finding the best franchisees. I went for regional directors in big corporate estate agents, who'd been there, done that, got the t-shirt, and who also had access to the initial franchise set-up fee.

What we really needed were dynamic and ambitious people who believe in the business's 'Why' and vision, which is what we have now attracted into the business, and it's working exceptionally well.

And this is only the start.

Hindsight is wonderful

When I look back on this story and see my journey from rugby captain to all the business ventures I have attempted, I can see recurring themes throughout.

It's all been about my 'Why', which is helping people. Whether assisting colleagues, clients or candidates, this attitude has been both my strength and my weakness along the way. My willingness and desire to help people means I have strung many people along for the ride who had no right to be on my journey. All of that said, it has been a learning journey, and I am now the person people look up to and want what I have. When I was 17 years old, Mark Barrow, my sixth form head, sat me down and said, "Josh, what do you want to do, really?"

I said, "Sir, I just want to wear a different designer suit every day, like you do, and drive a nice car like you do."

He said, "Stick that up on the wall, and you'll get there."

Another mentor, John Sims, asked me a similar question.

"Josh, where do you want to get to in life? We'll help you get there."

I said, "I want all the nice things in life. I want to run a business and want to be a leader because I care, and I want to help people."

I'm now in what I regard as a perfect situation, borne out of all the steps that have brought me to this moment: the discipline and competitiveness of rugby, the regimented schooling, the inspiring mentors, the constant entrepreneurial striving. Those aspects shine out for me.

I come from a serving mindset, and I want to bring people along for the journey. I've learnt that you can't be caged as an entrepreneur, and ultimately, nobody can box you in. However, I have also realised that I need people to work alongside me to help me learn.

I'll be the first person to admit that everyone on this planet has weaknesses, and I would say to anybody looking to follow a similar path to mine to find your own weaknesses early. Once you've done that, plug your weaknesses with good people that can stop the leakage. That philosophy has helped me hugely, as I've realised that I can't achieve success on my own.

When I look at the team I have built up around me now, I can point to specific strengths each team member has that plug the gaps I have in my own skillset. My lack of patience, which many will view as a positive, as I get stuff done, I also recognise is one of my worst traits. That's why I needed a management team that can support me and assist in planning, management and motivation to ensure that my business is profitable and successful.

I have always been bad at detail and the numbers, so I have needed a trusted ally who could run the money – step forward Rachael Gasson.

I needed strategy and business planning from someone who had been there and done it before and been mega successful – thank you Simon King.

I needed an operations and front-line support function that was second to none, headed up by a people person that really cared, someone who would do anything for anyone – take a bow, Jo Green.

I needed a leader, a trusted, loyal, loved and respected household name that had a clean sheet and was at the top of their game – who else but Estate Agency legend Russell Jervis.

Takeaways

- Don't take on too much

- Not everybody has your best interests at heart

- Plug your weaknesses (we all have them!)

- We can't grow alone

- Burnout is real

- Discover your purpose

- Assemble the right team around you

CHAPTER TWO

Is There Such Thing As Work/Life Balance?

Setting up and running any business requires absolute focus, hard work and, if you adhere to the stereotype, ridiculously long hours. In the early years of setting up my recruitment businesses, I sacrificed so much time and energy to ensure that each business was successful. This, unfortunately, resulted in never seeing my family from 7am – 7pm Monday to Friday. Even when I was physically present, I was on my phone answering emails at the local park, pushing my daughter Ruby on the swings while she screamed for attention.

When you are putting everything into a business initially, the burnout is real, and once it occurs, you'll be good for nothing outside of work. Without a good work/life balance, you *will* burn out – it's that simple. I was gently reminded of this fact by mentors, family and friends, who also mooted that I must actually *have* a business to achieve a work/life balance. Implying that I was working so hard, there may soon be no 'competent Josh' to run a business if I continued at such a pace. I have certainly learned how to lessen the load these days, but still, I am always the first one into the office and the last one out. I pride myself on always being available to add value to as many people as I can. I now realise, however, that without looking after myself properly, I won't be able to add the best value to clients or colleagues. So now, I do my best to spend as much time as possible on other key areas of my life.

This chapter will discuss what a good work/life balance looks like to me, what it potentially means for you, and the cultural work/life balance shift since the onset of the pandemic.

Freedom

When people set up a business, they usually do it for two reasons. The most common one is to be financially better off, and the other is to regain freedom and have more time for themselves. It is natural to want to go full speed ahead when you begin, but this is not a sustainable tactic. It's important to remember that one of the main objectives of having a business – in my opinion – is to have the freedom to spend time with your family, go to the gym, and explore your hobbies etc. Of course, money is a huge driver when setting up a business, but freedom is the ultimate goal. Money can deliver the latter.

In the early years, it's challenging to find a healthy work/life balance because usually, you're the one doing it all: you're the marketing director, the HR director, the sales director and the CEO. You do everything until you can scale, and it's exhausting. I've used the analogy over the years that you, your business and your personal life are a pizza. Four slices make up the pizza, and those slices have always been, for me, family, health, hobbies, and work. In the beginning, you are tasty and straight out of the oven, and everyone wants a piece of you, including your clients, your colleagues, your friends and family, and your health!

It's all-too common to head into your new business with tunnel vision but be mindful of how this can affect the people around you. Remember that your partner, children, parents and friends are the rock you are delicately balancing everything upon. It would be best if you made enough time for them *and* yourself, whether that's in meditation, fitness, hobbies, reading, or whatever makes you tick. You must make time for yourself, your family and friends, as *well* as your business. Working all day long is not sustainable for any person's physical or mental health. The bottom line is that if your mental health is not in check, you will let your fitness regime slide, or if you're not eating and sleeping correctly, you're not going to be able to work to the best of your abilities.

I am, regrettably, an authority on this subject because I got all of this totally wrong at the beginning of my business career. I had zero work/life balance. I was working all the time, and so I ended up completely ignoring my partner for a long while and missed out on some key moments of my eldest child growing up. During all those early trips to the park as a family and fun activities, I made excuses about how I needed to crack on with work. I can never get those moments back, and I regret that *deeply*.

Don't get me wrong, I still fall into bad old habits at times, but I am now conscious of it and make a determined effort to restore some balance. I still spend a bit too much time in the office as I pride myself on being available to add value to as many people as I can. However, I do my best to make sure that I spend as much time as possible in other areas of my life. But let's not pretend it's easy – it's difficult and it's complicated!

I began to look at it as a pyramid. I realised that my priorities were misaligned and, without the foundations of the pyramid in place such as my family, my self-improvement and my health, the whole structure would come tumbling down.

I look back and ask myself that if I hadn't had that out of alignment work-life balance early on in my career, would I have still achieved what I have? The resounding answer is YES! In hindsight, I worked hard, but I didn't work smart. Because I didn't have a solid academic background, I tried to make up for this by putting in the hours, and thus everything I learned was self-taught, which led to so many mistakes. I could have worked smarter and achieved a better work/life balance, but I thought I had to put in more hours than everyone else because I was feeling my way around in the dark.

How to work smarter

If I had had a mentor in my early life, or a workbook, a course, some sort of guidance, I think I would have arrived at some of these revelations on work/life balance much earlier than I did. But I didn't, and therefore I made some fundamental mistakes. I made the wrong business decisions and did things that wasted a huge amount of my time. If I had followed a strict process and my vision had been clear, I would have achieved my goals so much faster. Here, from my experience, are two key tools to help you to work smarter:

1: Be process-driven

Many people think, "I just want to have a great life. I want to drive nice cars, live in a big house and have nice holidays."

That's all good, but it's just part of the outcome. The journey to that outcome can be a long and arduous trek, and thus you must know *why* you want to get there. We will talk about finding our 'Why' later on, but first, I cannot emphasise enough how becoming more process-driven will help.

I was aware of processes when I started out, and I knew that others had previously laid out a roadmap, but I ignored all of that, deciding that I would do things my way instead.

When I worked briefly at my first recruitment job, I knew there were processes in place, but for me, at that time, it was just about growth and making money. Thus, I ignored all the boring backroom operation stuff and didn't take the time to study and implement due process. I knew in the back of my mind it was necessary but when you're starting up any business, getting the till ringing quickly is the overriding imperative. So, I chased the buck rather than investing in a system and following processes. We had in place a good state-of-the-art CRM and phone system, but in terms of the CX point, ie the customer journey from a client or candidate point of view, we should have road-mapped this in detail to make it much smoother and customer-friendly. On the one hand, I thought, "It's my way or the highway", and so I just didn't make the time to focus on this vital element. Instead, I was constantly on the phone, head down, building the business call by call, but letting processes slip as a result.

2: Harness online technology

Although I still consider myself a young man, the truth is that my work life straddles the onset of social media. When I started, there were far fewer online resources than are available today, like Google and LinkedIn, for example, weren't around early on in my career – can you now imagine recruiting without LinkedIn? The power of the internet, people's immediate access to online information and social media, has been a massive win for the recruitment industry. There are also all sorts of tools to help you find out so much about your market in detail. In just a few clicks, you can discover what your competitors are up to, what your clients are doing, and the profile of their customers. Now you can roadmap in amazing detail your niche or the sector you've identified as an opportunity, without even leaving your desk!

The internet is mighty. Previously, you wouldn't know anything about a candidate until they sent you a CV, but now you can go to their LinkedIn profile and understand their whole career journey before you even speak to them. I can now post a job online and have multiple candidates come back to me quickly, which has freed up so much time compared to traditional sifting. Now we are entering the era where you can listen to or participate in business podcasts in real-time about your niche or sector. I can only see that evolving even further, which will give people new to business much more due diligence and understanding as they take their first steps. We can use these tech tools to help us save time, make the process slicker, and free up more space for other life priorities.

The great contradiction though, as I'm sure we have all experienced, is that the internet, there to save us time with all the shortcuts (and more) I've just outlined and therefore free up our time, becomes a 'never off' tyranny, a 24/7 beast demanding our constant attention, all just at a quick glance down at our phones. This makes switching off and finding the right balance even more essential, as discussed below.

What the pandemic has taught the world about work/life balance

Although the subject had been mooted years before, during the pandemic people have had a powerful revelation that they wanted a better work/life balance. They realised that they really don't need to travel so much, and they would like, a few days every week, to drop and pick up their kids from school. Globally, it's clear that more and more people are demanding flexible working patterns to suit their lifestyle.

The pandemic has been truly dreadful, but I think we've learned a lot from it, and going forward, a good work/life balance will be more in play than ever before. People have realised that they are just as productive, if not more so, when working in the comfort of their own home or local office, rather than herding themselves into the major cities and towns, wasting time and money commuting, and ultimately being stressed out as a result. So, I am already hearing so many employers (and employees), asking, "Josh, what's the new normal? Is one day a week in the office okay? Are two days a week working at home acceptable?"

So many people are now opening their eyes, and candidates are asking for flexibility. I think all this will allow for a better work/life balance, whether two or three days a week, where you can be at home and can get up and use your Peloton for an hour and take the kids to school and work around your lifestyle. All compared to being in the car for over an hour, just wasting dead time. This new flexibility will allow all of us to be more productive and add more value to our families and our businesses.

Although many people have struggled during the pandemic, whether due to greater isolation or significant disruption to the business or their sector, but on the plus side, people have been able to spend quality time with their kids and spouses. They are now seeing their kids growing up and are realising, "I've been missing out on my own life!"

At the beginning of the pandemic, many people were embarrassed if the Zoom or phone call recipient could hear their kids in the background, and then – just like that – they stopped caring. It has become normal to be on a business call and hear kids running around, a dog barking or the postman knocking on the door. It's become normal to be in a professional conversation and yet with family life carrying on in the background. In my opinion, it has humanised business. There had always been the belief that people are less able to focus at home with family around, but the enforced change in ways of working brought on by the pandemic has blown that myth.

On the contrary, is that any more distracting than the myriad of stimuli in an office? However, of course, there needs to be a conversation in the household to clarify the boundaries: "This is my work time, this is my workspace". There must be an agreement that everyone in the home understands.

Of course, prioritising a work/life balance does not mean that you should put less effort into your business. For me, these days, it's all about 'organising the chaos'. I'm highly disciplined, so if something's not in my diary, I'm not going to be there, but if it's in the diary, I don't miss a beat. I'm a passionate person, and I love what I do. I relish getting to the office first, as I love that quiet time to settle into my working day. I also like to be available; whether that is speaking to people first thing in the morning in the car or last thing at night on the journey home, I'm always around if anybody needs to talk to me. Most of our competitors do a typical 9-5, and then they turn off, so my extra 'available' hours allow me to capture a corner of the market that my competitors don't. It also shows both the candidate and client that you're good at what you do, and that you don't mind putting the hours in to help them. Again, this comes back to my ultimate desire to help people find great jobs and assisting companies to find great people. If I'm on the phone at 7pm booking an interview, giving a candidate advice, or putting a job offer forward, doesn't that look better than my competitor who you can't get hold of after 5 pm? I think it does! Our industry is business owner-led, and they want to deal with people like themselves – entrepreneurial people who work hard to earn good money and give excellent service. So, intentionally, I have mirrored the way my audience works.

I don't in fact need to go to the office – it now runs itself, but I do love it! I like to be in the hustle and bustle of the shop floor. I missed it while we were all in lockdown, and I enjoy adding value to people in the office and our candidates and clients.

There are ways you can achieve optimum results at work and still achieve the perfect work/life balance.

For example, you can take that extra time in your day to jump on the Peloton while you take a call (although not if you're as unfit as me because you'll be panting down the line!). Or, like I did yesterday, I had an hour gap in my workday, so I played with the kids in the garden until I returned to my home office for a Zoom call.

The balance comes from having a smart and organised diary and managing it accordingly. If you can get out, get some fresh air, see your children and work on your fitness – yes, do it – because it will help you work with clarity. I look at my diary every day, and if there are gaps, I think, "What can I achieve with this free hour to address my work/life balance?"

It also helps to remember that it's not all about you and your success – it's likely you've got other people around you that need nurturing just as much as your business. If you don't have people around you, remember that you need to care for yourself. Remember the mantra, 'health before wealth'. There's no point in becoming the richest man in the graveyard. You need to invest in yourself because you won't have a business if you don't. That's what somebody kept telling me: "Josh, you're working all these hours, and you look grey in the face, mate! Go and have a holiday and switch off." It's essential to listen to the people around you when they make concerned comments like that. Prioritise your health and wellbeing, to become the best person to the people around you and the best person for your business.

Switching off

When thinking about work/life balance, many people believe they can fit everything in if they only get four hours of sleep a night, but that is a flawed approach. Proper sleep is imperative! I'm a bit of a baby, so I love to get an early night and sleep as much as possible. I'm in bed by nine o'clock most nights, and my alarm goes off at 5:30 am. That's my sleep pattern. Your pattern may be different, but whatever it is, try and stick to a regime to assure optimum energy and clarity for the next day.

I'm usually out like a light when my head hits the pillow, but if things keep me up at night, I always have a pen and pad next to my bed. If something is on my mind at night, I write it down, and I deal with it in the morning. If I've had a busy day and have forgotten to do something, it can wake me up. Rather than it being on my mind until the alarm goes off, I wake up, write it down, and then I go back to sleep. I can then switch off knowing that I can pick the book up in the morning, take it downstairs, and then action whatever I have written down.

When you first set up a business, you have so many creative, wild and wacky ideas on how you can change the world. Some of those ideas might be absolutely rubbish, but there might be some absolute gold in there too! So again, that pen and pad next to the bed is an excellent tool for calming an active mind. Write down your billion-dollar idea, sleep, and action it in the morning!

Don't get me wrong; I don't wake up every night and write an essay; it might be once a month, or even once every other month that I write something in there, but invariably, in the morning, it turns out to be a nugget worth having. Having a journal close at hand is a tool to tame all the thoughts flying around in your head and allows you to sleep.

So, an effective way to achieve that work/life balance is gaining and nurturing the ability to switch off. But, of course, a large part of being able to switch off is getting everything done you've promised to do. If you procrastinate, you will have more of a problem switching off at the end of the day and be less able to enjoy your quality time.

There is always a to-do list for a particular day, and that list will always increase throughout the day. Remember – there are always things on that list that can wait for another day. Ask yourself, "Shall I pick that up now? Is it life or death? Or can I pick it up in the morning?" If the latter is the case, then give yourself that time. This is different to procrastination – which is putting off things that need to be done. Choosing to leave something until tomorrow is prioritising. It's essential to know the difference.

Screen time

I mentioned earlier the potential 24/7 tyranny of the phone and I'm terrible for spending time on my phone, and I'm going to be transparent with you about my screen time. I'm looking at my stats now, and it states that I've spent an average of... eight hours and 45 minutes on my phone every day this week! That's ridiculous! I've shocked myself...

In my defence, I put my phone by my desk because I've got LinkedIn on there. I'm messaging people from the phone because I find it easier to tap away rather than use the keyboard, but eight hours and 45 minutes on average a day is too much, and that's just during my work day!

Now, even armed with the above information, I will get on my soapbox and advise that you should put your phone away for at least a few hours during your evenings and personal time. On Friday night, I ignored my own rule. I had spent ten hours during the day helping somebody and putting them into a job, and by the evening, they called to say that they were not going to take the job. If I hadn't answered, I wouldn't have known, and therefore it wouldn't have spoilt my mood and the precious time I have with my family. Discovering this on a Friday evening meant I couldn't react or resolve anything until the Monday morning anyway, but I dented my weekend needlessly by looking at my phone way after when I needed to!

So, not being able to put down work can affect your mindset and ruin your time outside of work. Some people advocate not looking at your phone for the first hour after waking up, and if that works for you, great, but I'm not one of them. I think, if you're a business owner, you need a medal if you can wake up and not look at your phone within the first hour! I'm a social person – I think most recruiters are too. I look at my phone in the morning to see if any family or friends have gotten in touch. I also want to understand what's going on in my industry before anybody else. We have a news feed called *Property Industry Eye*, which comes out at 7 am every morning. Very few people know (damn, they do now...), however, that they in fact release the stories at midnight. So, as soon as I get up at 5:30am, I look at the news on there. I get on the website straightaway, so I can comment and share that post. I become the influencer and the owner of that space first thing in the morning, and so when everyone else is sat on the train looking at their phones to get the news after 7am, guess whose name, share, and comment is popping up in front of them? My name! I use my phone as a tool to give me leverage against my competitors, but I do my best to put it away when it's time for my personal life.

Scaling

Doing things on your own, independently, is great if you want a lifestyle business and just like to run things the way you want to. Being a one-man-band suits many people, but if you want a work/life balance where you can go on holiday, or be ill for a week, and the business will still run itself, you need to scale, and you need to scale quickly. Scaling is all about increasing your headcount.

When you bring people in, you're initially investing a significant amount of time in training and making sure your team understands the systems and the processes etc., but that time will pay huge dividends in the future.

I wanted to build a business with the ultimate aim of being able to sell it, and I knew in the back of my mind that I could never just sell 'me', so I needed a business where I'm not 'in' the business, and instead I'm 'on' the business. If I remain the biggest fee earner, they would essentially be just buying me, and thus the business would be worthless. So, I needed to instill my knowledge and processes into all the people in my business to make sure it was valuable. Scaling is the way forward if you want to create a company worth selling.

A good work/life balance is something that we discuss in detail as a workforce. Our model is slightly different in that everybody is self-employed, and so we have 25 associates that work underneath our brand. Work/life balance is one of our selling points. We say, "You can join Rayner Personnel today: this is what you get from us, and this is what we expect. But this is your business, so build the business around you."

We have some working mums onboard who are great, they don't get to their desk till about half past nine because of school drop-offs, and they finish work at three o'clock because they have to do the school run. They pick up again after seven when the kids are in bed. It works for them, and it works for us. Our business model involves working with an individual to give them a work/life balance and allow them to be successful and earn the money they want to make. There's no pressure in regard to what they want to earn. We're very transparent and say, "If you put these hours in and trust in this process, you could achieve £££, and if you want to do double that, you can double the money. If you want to do half of what we suggest, then you can expect half the money. But we offer the work/life balance around your children and your current lifestyle."

As I mentioned in the last chapter, we have rebuilt our business in the previous 12 months, and who would have thought that we'd attract 25 people, all self-employed with no base salary for the first three months, in the middle of a pandemic? I didn't know it was possible, but people liked the proposition. Work/life balance is part of our USP when we are looking for people to join us, and it's been a hugely attractive element. It gives them flexibility, and people recognise that there is no such thing as security in employment or a job for life anymore. These days, people want to learn some skills for between 18 months and three years and then move on.

Offering a business opportunity to them means that they are in charge of their own destiny, and they haven't got a boss to be micromanaged by. There are no set KPIs, and we're in it as a partnership with the individual. So, as much as they put in, they're going to get out. People like that straightforward, honest approach because they understand that there is no longer such a thing as guaranteed job security as they have experienced big employers mistreating them, so why not back yourself rather than working for somebody else?

Of course, it depends on who you have been working for, but I think that the unprecedented disruption to our business and personal lives, caused by the pandemic, has resulted in a nerve-wracking time for everybody business-wise. When the pandemic first hit, especially here in the UK, people made knee-jerk reactions and are now being judged on those decisions. For example, there is one property business in the UK that no one will work for anymore because of how they dealt with their staff. They got rid of 400 people overnight before the furlough scheme was even announced, and now they are recruiting like crazy, and guess what – nobody wants to work there! So, as with that example, many people now realise that the security element of working for a larger business isn't there, and, on top of that, the tax structure doesn't work in their favour. If you earn £100K a year, you're only going to take home £50K, *and* you carry a huge burden of stress, much of which you cannot control. But now, people see that a better alternative is available, as we have shown with our model. Can you have a work/life balance, not have the KPIs and the monkey on your back (ie a big boss), *and* earn more money? Yes, you can!

Before, people would want to join a company because it was a blue-chip firm. With that, you would get all sorts of (taxed!) fringe benefits: life and health insurance, gym membership, a company car, and a high basic salary. But if you stand back and work out what you're doing, you're becoming a slave to a basic salary.

As a result, I think that so many more people are beginning to prioritise their work-life balance, and therefore we're going to see a massive shift in people going it alone or joining enterprises like ours. But, of course, there's still a large market for the traditional big business; that's never going to go away, and as a recruitment company we wouldn't want it to! There are still going to be high street operations, and there will still be a need for call centres etc., but I predict a significant shift towards the gig economy where people work for themselves. Whether that be as a lone ranger, or joining a business like ours, or taking on a retail franchise business like McDonald's, or a service franchise such as ActionCOACH or Molly Maid, more and more people have realised, after sitting at home for a year thinking, "Do I want to continue doing what I've been doing for so long?", the conclusion they have reached is "No, I don't!"

We did a mood survey, asking how many people wanted to go back to 'normal' after the pandemic. The results were fascinating. 60% of people didn't want to go back to their old job and their old way of working. People living in the big cities and towns have been saying this for years. They have sat at their desk, having just travelled an hour and a half to get into the office on tubes, trains, buses and walking in the snow, thinking, "There is no need for me to be sat here. I could be sat at home doing exactly the same thing."

As we advance, employers will need to change how they trust their employees, and both employers and employees will have to be honest and transparent. Employer and employee trust is also helped by the technology that is now available. For example, you can see how many times I make calls in and out every day, and I can see how many people are put on our system and how many interviews are going out. There is so much fantastic technology available to manage that process.

We have all been forced to get a study, add an extension or a garden office, or find a peaceful place in our homes where we can set up a desk. You can even see from the property market that having an office or desk space is now one of the biggest drivers when looking for a house.

All of that said, I still thrive on the office environment and the buzz, and I think many people feel the same way, so every week, we get together with our team to make sure they're all set up and happy. There's a bit of banter, and many people say it makes them feel like less of a recluse. I think a halfway house is to be had and while 100% based at home is fine, I think some people will suffer mentally, and some downright might not want it. It's morale-boosting to be cracking a few jokes with the whole team in the same room, a cup of tea in hand. People have had a lot of time on their own, and some have been suffering from isolation. If people live alone, most often they want to see other people – they need that contact. It's part of human nature.

What does work/life balance look like for me?

After initially thinking about this chapter, I did a thought experiment and asked myself what my ideal work/life balance looked like. I sat down and wrote it out without thinking too much, and here is what my subconscious said:

I'd love to spend more time with family, which means taking the kids to school every day, and that would be my routine. I'd like to get up, have breakfast, look at my emails, make some calls and then I'd take them to school. I'd love to do that! Failing that, I would at least like to pick the kids up from school. I want to take some time for myself, work on my fitness and do something in the day for an hour which is purely 'Josh time'. I would also like to invest in myself, whether attending a seminar, watching a guest speaker, or listening to a podcast. I want to put in a daily routine which will help my family life, make me happier, and help my business life. If I'm spending more time on myself, whether that be meditation, going to the gym, or however I get my endorphins up, that will only be a good thing for home AND business. That is what a work/life balance looks like to me.

What about you?

We have discussed the benefits, and the whys and whatnots of a work/life balance, and I am sure you agree that this balance is imperative to success in all areas of our lives. So, why don't you try the exercise that I did above? Ask yourself, "What does a work/life balance look like to me?"

Try to visualise what it would look like if you had a finely tuned work/life balance. Once you have a clear vision, you can start to summarise your priorities. Ask yourself this question in stages, over time:

1)   What would be an ideal work/life balance for next week?
2)   What would an ideal work/life balance be for next month?
3)   What would an ideal work-life balance be for next year?
4)   What should it look like when I'm 50 years old, 60 years old, even 70 years old?

These answers will help you prioritise and make the right decisions. Getting your work/life balance right could be the recipe for all your future success.

Takeaways

It's important to remember that one of the main objectives of having a business – in my opinion – is to have the freedom to spend time with your family, go to the gym, and explore your hobbies etc. Of course, money is a huge driver when setting up a business, but freedom is the ultimate driver.

- Follow processes to avoid dead time

- Use tech tools to save time, make processes slicker, and free up space for other life priorities

- There are ways you can fully achieve at work and also have an outstanding work/life balance

- Whatever your sleep pattern, stick to a regime to assure optimum energy and clarity for the next day

- If you want a work/life balance where you can go on holiday, be ill for a week, or the business runs itself, you need to scale

CHAPTER THREE

What Drove My Success – Big-Picture Thinking

What is big-picture thinking?

Go big, but not too big. Be a disruptor, understand your market, do your research, do your due diligence, come up with your vision and then build a plan around it.

Believe me on this – I didn't know any of this when I started, and I wasted a *lot* of time.

My WHY

I have included an entire chapter dedicated to 'discovering your Why', but I want to touch on it briefly here, as it's an integral element of big-picture thinking. I knew I wanted to create a nationally recognised brand that provided a first-class service for candidates *and* clients, like had never been offered before. But then I had to ask myself, "Why, fundamentally, are you actually doing any of this?"

Of course, there are the holidays, the watches, the cars and the lifestyle that go hand-in-hand with success. But, if you haven't got your 'Why' right, all you're doing is lying to yourself and your customers. My Why is that I want to help people. To discover this, I had to grab the proverbial onion, pull back the layers and think, "If I build my business around what I'm passionate about, it will be a lot better received, and I can do a better job."

How to use USPs

I have used clever technology as one of my USPs. Harnessing technology, along with the hard grunt work that other recruiters don't want to do, including loads of cold calls, sifting through thousands of CVs, and late nights profiling candidates, have all been the norm for me. Technology, when used properly, is a game-changer. As a headhunter, people are paying me to do a service that they don't want to. Just like when I need to paint my house, I get a decorator round because I'm rubbish at painting and I haven't got the time to do it. So, when you need someone to do the stuff you don't want to do, you call in a professional.

To differentiate our business, we also use psychometric profiling–benchmarking. To do that, we use a nifty bit of kit called 'McQuaig'. This gives you three levels of an individual's profile. It can tell you whether a person is dominant or social, and you can map out the person you are speaking to and understand what their drivers are. There's no point putting a driven person into an admin job because they will just leave, and neither the candidate nor client will ultimately get anything from that. Using psychometric profiling, we test both the client and the candidate to make sure we know precisely the right candidate for the role. Office cultures and candidates with similar profiles will get along because their personalities match. McQuaig provides a guaranteed 96% match compared to the usual 50% fit. This saves us and our clients a huge amount of precious time!

Another USP we have is to screen people using video interviews – and yes, we did this even before the pandemic! Back in 2013, we were using video even before the iPhone had a front-facing camera or webcams were integrated into laptops. At one point, I sent webcams out to candidates to attach to their computers so that they could produce videos of themselves – I feel I'm showing my age now! So, technology has always been a large part of my businesses.

For headhunting, we use a website that allows us to find out market share of the players in our specialist market sector, the property industry. So, if I put in 'Clapham, London', for example, it gives me a Yellow Pages-style directory of every estate agency business in Clapham. And then if I click 'switch', it gives me a ranking of one to 20 by market share of each of these, based on how many properties they have currently got on the market to sell. Typically, the agents with the most stock – guess what – produce the most amount of revenue. This then gives us a league table of who the top agents are. So, for example, if our customer is number five and they're looking for a branch manager, there is no way the branch manager from the first two or three firms will want to move backwards to run another business with lower revenues. So, we are able, instead, to target more precisely where we need to seek the best candidates for that role.

As a result, these technologies allow you to cherry-pick and approach the right people, rather than the scattershot approach I was trained in early in my recruitment career: "Just ring everyone Josh and ask if they want a new job!"

I wasted thousands of man-hours in the past when instead, armed with the correct information I could have just made four phone calls, four LinkedIn requests or four social media messages. Technology makes it so much easier and precise to search for the right candidates. We also use mystery shopping techniques with the mapping tool. We would walk the high street visiting estate agency branches, pretending to buy or let a property, to judge the quality of customer experience being received. This allowed us to pinpoint which agencies were providing a good service, and which ones were weak.

We are almost always confident that we have placed the right person once we have qualified them over the phone, by video, and have then requalified them using the psychometric profile. Our track record, and excellent client feedback, has proven to us that this process ensures that when we do make a placement, it actually sticks, and in that way, we are providing a valuable service to our candidates and our clients.

As I have said, it was back in 2013 when I started harnessing new technology. That was already halfway into my career, and I noticed the difference immediately. Technology soon became one of our main USPs.

In the early stages of my career, when I was working for a recruitment company, you would approach a candidate during the working day, but of course they couldn't speak in the office because they had a boss breathing down the back of their collar. So, you would always ask them for a mobile number and give them a call between seven or eight o'clock that evening once they had got home from work. I would then spend 20 minutes or more with each candidate going through their background, qualifying them for the role, understanding the most significant drivers and motivators for them to move. If they would consider a move, what does it look like? I would go through all their performance numbers and figures, their basic salary, their commission structures, and then basically sell them a role that I thought would be suitable. I remember coming home from work every day; Mum would put dinner on the table, we all sat around the dinner table, and I was literally stuck on my old phone. The looks I got over the table were interesting. That happened every single night for about three years. So, I did most of my work outside of the 9-5 working day, when people could have a conversation with me.

When I had my first recruitment firm, it was more challenging to find ways to differentiate back then. Like most recruitment companies, you just went onto Indeed and Reed, did a quick CV search, chucked loads of CVs at the wall and hoped some of them would stick. That was as scientific and systematic as it got! But this wasn't helping our reputation as a recruitment business because everyone was doing that. We have so moved on from such a wasteful and unfocused approach, with technology being harnessed to help us distinguish our business.

Trying to take on the universe and realising it's HUGE!

I wanted to change my industry for the better. I tried to change what had been done before, and that's when I had the idea of 'Estate Agency All-Stars' as I mentioned in the first chapter. With the clever technology (psychometric profiling and video interviewing), I offered a screening process never seen before from a recruitment company in the property space. I then went one step further. Once the candidate was successful, I put them through an industry-leading five-day training course on the basics. This included uploading a property on Rightmove, developing questioning tactics, being clear on the consumer journey, understanding compliance etc. The course was an industry first, and only the prominent corporate agents offered such a course to newbies.

To circle back a little bit, Rayner Personnel is an executive search business, so somebody with two to four years' experience plus is our bread and butter; essentially, people who can fee-earn and generate income. But, outside of that box, I thought that there was a huge, unexploited niche for junior recruitment in the property sector. At the time when Rayner Personnel started, everyone was putting a free ad on Indeed or placing an advert in a local paper, and all this was yielding was unsuitable, inexperienced people. Once they took up the job, the clients weren't providing them with the necessary support and training to plug that inexperience, and so, all too often those candidates were soon leaving. The clients then didn't want to pay the recruitment fee for those now ex-employees, because it seemed to be a waste of money. That fee would be a percentage of the candidate's basic salary. And yes, I agree that paying £4,000 for a junior who doesn't stay isn't a great idea. So that's where All-Stars came from. We screened each person using their profile in the video. If suitable we would then offer them a job, but before they started, we would put them through a five-day induction. The induction would explain what an estate agent is, the rules and regulations of the industry, what software platforms to use, how to understand your customers, and all the other groundwork that you that don't get from an independent estate agent. I think you would probably agree that if you started at Virgin or BA, you would be offered a thorough training programme to ensure that the foundations were laid correctly to allow you to grow.

Whereas in estate agency, all too often, you would get a job and merely sit next to 'Johnny'. You would watch and learn from him, and everything you knew would be either self-taught or from Johnny. So, I thought, "If it is only the corporates who are offering training, how can I exploit that void in the market?" The idea was to offer recruitment alongside the training school. We received great feedback. The students were placed as juniors in estate agency offices ready-made with the equivalent of six months' experience rather than just being straight off the street. We had some excellent success, and the candidates felt good because they went into estate agents' offices knowing the basics, the buzzwords and the terminology. Sure, they weren't a finished article by any means, but they knew about Rightmove (which was the largest portal), they learned about applicants and how to screen them correctly with the right questioning. They knew the basic stuff without being taught it in a traditional independent estate agency setting. So that was successful to a certain degree. It was different, and unique – no one else was doing anything like that. I remember driving past several estate agency businesses and they all had in their windows the staff certificates I'd given to them. They were advertising in the local newspaper saying, "We invest in our staff – we have put them through an industry training course". They hadn't – they had just paid me, and I had done it – but employers liked the fact that they appeared to be adding value. Of course, I used that as a USP to attract more people to my business.

After candidates had finished the course, we asked them to fill out a feedback questionnaire, which we then revisited after three and six months. The feedback was always positive. The course got them into a classroom with other people of a similar age, also starting their journey in estate agency, and we created a community. The students were with like-minded people, of similar backgrounds and age, all which made the classes fun and engaging. Inevitably, after the course, a few of the trainees, once they got into an estate agent's office found that they didn't like the job or industry, but most of them flew and loved it.

I believed I had cornered the market, by having both a junior offering and Rayner Personnel for more senior candidates. But like most people, I found it hard to juggle both businesses. I sold All-Stars, and my calmness and demeanour improved immeasurably. Before, I was running around worrying about bits and pieces, from dropping off laptops to a training course to ensuring the trainer had turned up, to constant board meetings with the guy from the review website. By selling the All-Stars business, I had all that extra stress taken away from me. It was a breath of fresh air, and it was a massive relief to concentrate on one thing.

I'm passionate about recruitment: that's my background. The other stuff was the bells and whistles and the icing on the cake, but it just didn't work. I failed and failed quickly, got rid of that problem, and now I've never looked back!

Big picture thinking

It starts with your vision and *then* your plan.

Your vision is what you set out, and what you want to do. Where are you going? Have you got a three-year plan, a five-year plan, a ten-year plan? What is your vision for your future personally and your business?

Vision

My vision for Rayner Personnel is:

I've got a five-year plan because that takes me up to 40, and when I'm 40, I want to be sitting on a beach. So that's my ticking clock. I want to be the number one property-based recruitment business in the UK via a licensed network. And we are going to support 25% of the market with executive search property recruitment.

It is essential that you research your vision in some detail – the marketplace, the current operators in it, the sector, likely clients, the growth potential, a whole range of factors. All this will confirm whether you're doing the right or wrong thing, and it will guide your journey. Your research will help shape your vision, but it must still come from the heart and reflect a passion you have. You can't just think, "My mate John has a great recruitment business, and I want to be just like him. I want to drive a nice car like he does!"

That won't work. You must conduct detailed research and make sure there is a market for your vision and that you will enjoy the work.

Plan

The plan is examining how you are going to achieve your goals. For me, currently, in outline it is:

Building a sustainable and valued business. Growing the business to £10m turnover.

And I have then built a detailed three-year plan around that, which I lay out in more detail in Chapter 11. It is a solid, achievable plan, with all the strategy and detail in place to ensure our ambitious financial target is reached by the target date.

How do I know if there is a market for my dream job/business?

The internet provides so much data, from government reports to the ONS (Office of National Statistics). The ONS analyses salary data from different sectors and, interestingly, how much each sector is worth and how many people are hired in each different sector.

I look at things from a perspective of recruitment, but even if my sector is not one related to your vision, there is so much useful information you can find out that will relate to any industry or marketplace. For example, if you tie up with a recruitment body (I use the REC, the Recruitment Employment Confederation), but there is also The British Institute of Recruiters, they will give you inside data on temps, contracts, permanent staff levels, and how many people they've hired each year. That will help you understand what market to go in and what the most lucrative markets are. LinkedIn is also a great source of intel and, guess what, there are kind people out there that will meet you for a coffee to discuss their knowledge – don't be afraid to ask! You're the new kid on the block and not expected to know everything.

Once you have conducted all this detailed research, you can tie this into your vision to check that it is going to work.

What can you realistically achieve?

When looking at your vision, look at your plan, and decide:

1) what's an achievable plan?
2) what are your stretch goals?
3) what wouldn't be a good outcome?

Work out an honest picture of where you could take the business.

Map it out and say, if I hit 'a', it will be great, if I hit 'b', it will be amazing, and if I don't achieve my vision in the way I expected, and 'c', work out the extent of the downside and work out what action you would potentially need to take. You have got to be realistic in the early days because things don't always go to plan, but always remember what your USPs are and return to them when you feel like you are drifting.

How do I recognise my own USPs?

Research, research, research!

How are you different to anybody else in the marketplace? You can find out that answer with research. Try mystery shopping with your competitors, reading the trade magazines and online journals, follow what people are doing. In the case of my industry, I am continually looking at who is hiring and analysing the ways in which they are hiring.

So, let's look at what I do as an example. Everyone in my industry says they're a headhunter, so I had to break down what this exactly means to discover my USPs. I'm a headhunter, sure, but there are reasons we don't just ring up people and say, "Do you want a job?" Instead, we carry out a deep dive into market share analysis and performance analysis. We identify the correct individual; we then do our research and background check into that individual before making contact. We spend an hour and a half on the phone to understand their key attributes, skillset and behaviours, and performance. We then spend the time producing a video profile of that individual. And after that, we benchmark their psychometric profile to make sure that we understand that candidate 360°. We then matchmake that candidate to the perfect job because, critically for us, we don't get paid any money if they don't stay in the role.

We guarantee three months' job tenure, so if someone takes up a position and it doesn't work out within the first three months, no questions, no quibbles, you, as the company who took us on to fill the position, get your money back. If they don't work out, for whatever reason, we can then organise providing a suitable replacement candidate for the role, free of charge. This is a guarantee that we are confident in offering, in that we know what we're doing, and we know we will find the right candidate for the organisations that use us. But, of course, human beings can change their mind. Even after the detailed and rigorous process we go through to ensure that the best candidate fills each role, curveballs happen. They might suddenly fall ill, and if they now live in London in their new role, they might have to suddenly move back home and thus quit their new job. The unexpected happens. But we are always satisfied that, through our detailed processes and research, we have matched the candidate to the role in the best possible way, and better than our competitors could.

Again, in our sector, I realised that there are so many ways to stand out, all of them better than the mainstream, accepted approach from employers of "Here's a job spec Mr Recruiter, go and fill it, and then invoice me." For us, we have explored breaking the mould and offering a subscription model or a 'pay on success' structure, or a retained option. In your own sector there will be so many things you can do to be unique in your market space and finding those USPs comes down to doing your research.

Have your WHY at the centre of everything you do

It's easy to get blindsided when you set up your business. For example, you might have a massive cash demand to keep the business going, and therefore need to grow. In recruitment, it's very tempting to chase the money because it's often hand-to-mouth when you start. I know from first-hand experience, however, that if you chase the money, it never comes. If you cut corners – guess what – you cut your service, and you're not as successful. Make sure that you do the right things at the right time, which, in our sector, results in adding real value to both the candidate and the client. My Why is to help people find great jobs, have great lives, and find great people for companies to help them have great lives. I have my Why aligned in everything I do, and thus I always offer the proverbial 'Red Carpet Rayner Service'. Our values at Rayner all concern relationships and reputation. We make sure that everything we do aligns with our Why.

If, again in our sector, you just want to try to get rich quick by banging in loads of CVs indiscriminately, just playing a numbers game, then frankly, you will never find a USP that will allow you to sustain in our marketplace – your service levels just won't stand out. To avoid this approach, you need to keep reminding yourself of your Why. You might then realise, if you stand back and look honestly at your own business, that you have lost sight of your vision and instead are just chasing short-term money. The worst end result of that can be that you end up with crappy fees, offering a crappy service and actually, you have a crappy business. And no one wants that.

Your Why is something bigger than yourself, and you should try to keep perspective on exactly why you're headed in that direction and not let go of your values.

Purpose over popularity

It's natural to want to do every bit of PR, that every single marketing video and piece of social content out there should become popular, but if you haven't got a purpose, it's going to fail.

Everybody wants to be popular. We're all human beings, and we all want to be liked, but your purpose must be the driving factor. The popularity will come once you've done the job and you've done it well; then, people will come back to you.

You see many people launch a new business who think, "I'm the best thing since sliced bread!" They have such big egos that they can't get in the room, and they are seldom successful because their purpose isn't central.

In my sector, I've seen many recruitment companies come and go due to putting popularity over purpose. Maybe they start out by offering loads of giveaways, or they slash their fees so low and undercut everybody else that it seems like a no-brainer from a customer's point of view. They're doing that merely to buy market share and come to believe they have won popularity, but there is no foundation to it, no genuine loyalty or true popularity. At the margins at which they are operating, the service is inevitably affected, and it is just not sustainable.

A good example in our sector is the springing up of third-party CV search companies, that offer to find a candidate for just £500. All they do is a quick CV grab, and then the client has to do the hard work of sifting through them all. They are only performing a small percentage of the recruitment process, just the start-point of getting the CV in front of the client, and then the client is having to do the rest. These companies are setting out to buy popularity through a headline-grabbing attractive price point and change the industry in the process. Unfortunately for them, once clients see beyond the headline, they are soon realising that there is no quality of service in place – you do indeed get what you pay for.

In summary

Don't think you can do more than you can.

Sure, you want to take on the universe, but so does everyone else in the world. Be realistic. Big-picture thinking isn't about thinking big; it's about understanding your market and being truthful with yourself. Human beings can do so many amazing things, but be pragmatic, think outside the box, and don't blindly follow the norm. If you're going to be different, you need to disrupt the market.

Go big, but not too big. Be a disruptor, understand your market, do your research, do your due diligence, come up with your vision and then build and execute a plan around it.

Takeaways

- Decide upon what you can realistically achieve

- Discover your USPs

- Discover what you are doing differently to anybody else in the marketplace

- There are many things you can do to be unique in your market space and finding those USPs comes down to doing your research

- Have your Why at the centre of all you do

- You must place your purpose above popularity

CHAPTER FOUR

Your Why

In life, you never know when lightbulb moments will occur. Whether in the middle of the night, chatting with your friend, or sitting on a train, it's impossible to know when you will get a tangible "aha!" moment.

My Why began with a person and a book

Well, to be precise, it started with an inspirational person giving me an equally inspirational book and then assisting me in applying the content to my own life. The book was *Start with Why* by Simon Sinek, and the person that gave me the book was Michael Bruce. I owe both of those people a great deal.

Michael and his brother Kenny are business associates of mine. I used to place the majority of the staff at their company, Purple Bricks, and I have always got on well with them both. I tend to respect people that have done well and trodden the path that I want to tread in the future, and naturally, I always get a little blown away when I meet those people. So, with that in mind, I was pleased when Michael called me and said, "Josh, I would love to invite you over to my house."

Michael and Kenny had set up a new business called Boomin, which has just launched here in the UK, see Boomin.com, 'The game-changing property search', so I guessed it was to do with that.

"Brilliant," I thought, "he wants some more staff for his new business."

I arrived at his house of which is a large property and rather extravagant. I rolled up and took my shoes off.

"You don't need to take your shoes off, just come in," he said.

"No, I'm respectable," I said nervously as he made me a coffee.

We then had a tour of his fantastic property. Oh, on a side note, everybody I know who is super-rich – like £20 million-plus – all have a bar in their house. Sort of a man-cave. I'll take this minor observation to mean that I will know I've *really* made it when I get the obligatory man-cave bar!

After the epic house tour, we sat in the dining room, with about a hundred chairs around the table and a giant whiteboard with my name on it.

"Wow, this guy's put some prep into this business proposition!" I thought.

"So, I brought you here, Josh", he begins, "to give you a mentoring session."

Err, what?? I was not expecting that! However, as soon as I understood the reason I had been personally summoned to his mansion, I was thrilled.

Great, he must see something in me!

He asked me lots of questions about my business, such as my projections, and what I turn over, etc. We've got a mutual respect and trust, so I didn't mind sharing. After that storm of questioning, he paced up and down the room for two hours. Just up and down, up and down, up, down, up, down. Eventually, he asked me this question:

"Why are you doing what you want to do?"

Why are you doing what you want to do? That's an odd question. Oddly worded, yet strangely enticing.

And that was the moment, the precious moment in time when the penny dropped for me. That is when my Why revealed itself.

People will tell you to read loads of books and listen to endless podcasts, but I think it's challenging to listen to them or read all those books when you've got a busy life. But, when Michael gave me the Simon Sinek book, I took it and I decided to read it. If he was recommending it, it must be a significant book. He had underlined the parts he deemed important for me and had written notes.

Back to the pacing. He broke me down for two hours before landing his question, "Why are you doing what you want to do?"

I wanted to answer authentically.

I said, "I want to have a great life; I want to drive nice cars. I want to have nice holidays. I want to build a business that I can potentially sell in the future."

He kept digging away, so much so that I felt like I was in an army interrogation room with a sack over my head. At first, I didn't know what he was trying to do. I was trying to answer the questions as you normally would. But when it got down to his key question, "Why are you doing what you want to do?" I suddenly realised what my true answer was, and the words tumbled out:

"It's to genuinely help people."

"Ahh – there you go, Josh! You want to help great people find great jobs and great companies find great people," he said.

"Yeah, absolutely!"

He was trying to get me to focus down on the centre of what I'm doing and **why** I'm doing **what** I'm doing.

I didn't fully reach that conclusion there and then, however. He told me to go away, really think about it and come back a week later.

I had mixed emotions when the idea started to cement in my mind, and I was angry at myself.

Oh my God, why didn't I think of that earlier? I could have been a lot more successful by now if I'd known my Why before!

Michael broke it down for me: "If you do things right, and you put your Why at the centre of everything you do, the 'how' and the 'what' come after. Of course, you want nice holidays, nice cars, and you want your kids to go to a private school, but if you concentrate on that first, you're never going to get there."

The chat with Michael was an inspiring and important two hours of my life. I went home and sent him a bottle of champagne to say thank you for his time.

He had a massive wine rack there with about a hundred bottles of Dom Perignon, but I clocked one bottle missing as I looked around. Along with the Dom Perignon, I also sent a video message:

"Thank you so much for your time; I appreciate it. You have helped me to truly discover my Why."

Now, every time I get some success, I share it with him, as I feel he deserves to know how much he has inspired my shift in mindset.

As for our Why as a business, this can be summarized as follows:

Our message is simple – we help people find great companies and companies find great people. In turn we assist candidates, clients and each other to have amazing lives.

Your Why

Just as Michael has helped me, it would be an honour for others to read this book and discover their own Why.

It's natural to want the 'what' – which is the stuff you get when you do a good job. The 'what' is the lifestyle stuff: the holidays, cars, and the other material things. It's important to remember that these things come and go. They're just the bells and whistles that you'd like to have. Of course, any entrepreneur wants a great lifestyle that will go hand-in-hand with what they're trying to do, but, in my opinion, the true motivation is a bug, something unquenchable that you MUST do. When you're really passionate about what you do and get your Why absolutely nailed down, you get so much more from that than you do from the 'what'.

We are worth more than the work we do, and the work we do is supposed to reflect who we are and what our worth is.

I think many people go through their life without nailing down their clarity on their Why. I was almost one of them. Of course, you naturally want to build a business. You want to inspire people. You want to help people, but if you don't have your Why crystal clear, that can be disastrous.

Even if your Why is discovered, it can be so easily forgotten. We live busy lives where everything is a couple of clicks away, and there are so many things happening, with their attendant pressure and stress. So, sometimes you need to bring yourself back to "Why do I do what I do?"

By asking that question and reminding yourself of the answer, you can gain back the enjoyment in all your endeavours too.

After the meeting with Michael, I got wholly stuck into ensuring my Why was crystal clear, yet simple and easy to remind myself about. I probably spent a week concentrating almost exclusively on it, it is that important I ran it past the directors in the business, I ran it past my wife and my family, and it helped me clarify what I'm trying to do. Those outside influences helped me to discover where I wanted to take my business and my life.

How to differentiate your WHY from your HOW and your WHAT

To help to understand this, I strongly recommend you look at Simon Sinek's Golden Circle as a clear illustration of the relationship between Why, How and What. His Golden Circle has three concentric circles, with Why in the centre, How in the next circle outwards, and finally What in the outer circle.

Put simply, your **Why** is the reason you are on your endeavour; your **How** is the mechanisms you need to put in place to get there; and the **What** are the things you will acquire and achieve as a result.

The **Why** is the hardest part, but the **How**, at least in recruitment, is all about relationships that instill trust. We obviously get CVs over to clients and we do that through job boards, headhunting, LinkedIn and social media, but ultimately, it's all about the importance of great communication and working with each other.

At Rayner Personnel, we have created a detailed two-day induction for every single person that joins our business. In the morning we get them to speak about their **Why**, and goal setting. Once we have established those things, we can build a framework around them. From the offset, we establish their **Why**, and we reinforce our **Why**, as that is at the heart of the motivation within our business. It gets people thinking. They need to believe in their **Why** and they have to jump on board with ours.

The typical **Whys** that we hear are: "I want to have a nice lifestyle – I want my kids to have a good life and go to private school."

But these are not **Whys**, they are byproducts – these are **Whats** – not the heartstrings of the **Why**.

Of course, everybody in our sector wants to be the best recruitment company, but how do you become the best so that people buy into your **Why** rather than the product? To answer that, you must drill down to the deep core of the **Why**.

How do you communicate your Why to a wider audience?

You can communicate your Why by being honest, authentic, following the process, doing the right things by people and not simply chasing the money! Money-chasing damages reputations, and ultimately therefore, their Why is never fulfilled. In our sector, we need to constantly ask ourselves, are we doing the right thing by both the candidate and by the client? And if the answer is no, we don't do it. You need to find the equivalent benchmark questions in your sector and must be strict and ruthless about asking them all the time. Look after your reputation, because if you haven't got a good reputation, you haven't got anything.

This goes for the whole team too – great people equal great companies. If you have somebody onboard that doesn't fit your Why, then it isn't a good look for your brand and business. Be selective with whom you choose to represent your brand. We have a three-person selection before we take anybody on. If any of the three say no to the potential new person, then it's a no from the whole business. We all need to resonate with each other and know that we are all running the same race. We get the right people in the right seat.

The **Whats** are wonderful, of course, but they are not what you will be thinking about as you finally get to that point near the end of your life.

You won't be thinking about what you owned – you will be thinking about what you valued, who you helped, and what difference you made in the world.

Takeaways

- Why are you doing what you want to do?

- If you do things right, and you put your **Why** at the centre of everything you do, the **How** and the **What** follow on

- Your **Why** is the reason you are on your endeavour; your **How** is the mechanisms you need to put in place to get there; and **What** are the things you will acquire and achieve as a result

- You can communicate your **Why** by being honest, authentic, following the process, doing the right things by people and not simply chasing the money!

- The **Whats** are wonderful, of course, but they are not what you will be thinking about as you near the end of your life

CHAPTER FIVE

Wedded to Growth

Being wedded to growth, at the heart of this notion, is all about passion. When you set up a business, you want to grow it because you want to be successful, and you enjoy all the nice things that come with success. But you must be wedded to it; ergo, be in love with it. You must make sure that you're working hard to make your business successful. Many people who set up a business can be a little flighty at the beginning. Sometimes that comes from having too many ideas up in the air, but on occasion it's because they don't want to concentrate on it. Maybe it's simply a hobby, and guess what, that never usually goes anywhere. Being wedded to growth is the key to the success of the business.

> *If you're going to embark on setting up a business, you must give it your all.*

What does wedded mean?

Being wedded to growth requires that you live and breathe your business and always look for improvements in the way that it is working. It's not a vacation or a pick it up and put it down when you wish scenario; you must work hard at it every single day to make sure it's successful.

You must be passionate about your business, and you've got to want it. Think of wedded as you would in the way you would in a relationship with your other half. I use the word 'wedded' similarly to imply that it's a commitment you make to your business in the same way you would in a loving and committed relationship.

"For that reason, I'm out"

James Caan is a hugely successful recruitment guru; he has sat on *Dragons' Den* in the UK, has bought and sold many businesses, and is a multi-multimillionaire. In 2013, when I first started Rayner Personnel, I saw a link on LinkedIn that read:

> *"Do you want £500,000 worth of investment, and a guru like James Caan to grow your business?"*

I was immediately hooked in! I applied to become a recruitment entrepreneur. I put a big presentation forward, and there were 30,000 other applications. The first stage was an interview. I had to go down to Mayfair and was interviewed by the recruitment entrepreneur CEO. I breezed that. The second stage was where they asked for my business plan for the next three to five years. Together with them, we were working as a team to put together a three-year plan. Then we talked about where we would be based. We went to different premises, and they sold me the idea of working in fantastic locations. Finally, I met their marketing team, who discussed building me a website. I was treated like a member of the team, and so it was not a huge surprise that from the 30,000 applicants, I was chosen as the elected candidate. That was when James Caan personally invited me to his board room so I could make my final presentation.

"Josh, we loved you and the presentation. You were amazing," he said afterwards.

I was nervous and buzzing.

James then said, "We'd like to offer you the £500,000."

I'd only gone and won half a million pounds' investment with one of the world's most successful and famous entrepreneurs! However, there was a catch...

"We will give you £500,000, but we want 75% of your business. We will also need you to move to London, and you will have to take a pay cut initially."

Apart from the money, these were all the things that I didn't want to do. I especially didn't want to lose a controlling interest in my business. I also had a young family, and I didn't want to move to London or travel to London every day.

It was amazing up until that point – talk about an experience! Smoking cigars in the board room, a personal butler bringing champagne, hummus and peppers. James stood there with an outstretched hand, with a cheque for half a million quid.

"But you're not going to shake my hand, are you, Josh?"

"No", I said, "I'm not going to take your offer."

I know you probably think I was crazy for not taking the offer during such early days at Rayner Personnel but hear me out! For me, at that time, it wasn't worth the investment, but it was great to have gone through the recruitment entrepreneur experience to the investment stage, especially with James Caan who has been there and done it all.

"Josh," James said, "I know that you want to scale your business but remember that only 10% of UK recruitment companies have over ten people in them."

I already knew this, but I listened intently. James continued.

"So, if you want to grow a business, do you just want to be a lifestyle business? Of course, there is nothing wrong with being niche and doing it all in your back bedroom. But, if you want to be a serious player, you need to recruit ten people plus and be on the right growth plan going forward. This investment and my involvement will help."

"James, I am so grateful, but..." I began.

James cut me off. "There is somebody in line right behind you that will jump at this chance if you don't take it."

He wasn't lying – my biggest competitor took the investment. Of course, taking the £500,000 probably would have accelerated my growth far quicker, but then you've got to weigh up and balance the 75% of equity I would have lost. When I rejected his offer, he said he accepted my decision.

I am often asked if I regret that decision. I don't. Everything in life happens for a reason, I believe, and it was the right decision at that time for me going forward. I would have been somebody else's puppet and not my own man. I was wedded to my *own* plan and growth instead of jumping on someone else's bandwagon.

We all have the same time in a day

There are only eight working hours in a typical day, and I appreciate that when you set your business up, you'll want to work 12, even 14-hour days to get it going, but as we discussed you'll quickly burn out doing that! At some point you should get your hours to a sensible weekly pattern. By doing that, you need to surround yourself with people to take up the other hours that you can't commit to. Remember that you've got other commitments to family, friends, hobbies and interests.

I was taught early on, especially with the James Caan scenario, that "you're only one person, Josh, and you're only as good as your last deal. To get more value and more revenue out of what you're doing, you need to get more good people around you."

First Who – getting the right people on the bus – then What, is a concept developed in the book *Good to Great*:

'Those who build great organizations make sure they have the right people on the bus and the right people in the key seats before they figure out where to drive the bus. They always think

first about who and then about what. When facing chaos and uncertainty, and you cannot possibly predict what's coming around the corner, your best "strategy" is to have a busload of people who can adapt to and perform brilliantly no matter what comes next. Great vision without great people is irrelevant.'

Jim Collins

I love this concept. I interpret it to mean that everyone should have a collective vision, and that it's better to have nobody rather than the wrong person. You should get the right person with the right energy, the right background and the right traits, and who has bought into your vision. If you get a bad apple, it can affect the rest of the team. Growth is about getting more people involved, true, but it's essential to pick the right people. The wrong person will slow you down and stunt your growth. So, to paraphrase Jim Collins, to get you there faster, focus on getting the right people in the right seat, on the right bus with the same collective vision.

You'd think the fact that I work in recruitment would mean I am more attuned to who would be a good fit for my team, but I can't say that this has always been the case. You'd be surprised; when it's your own business, you can make some haphazard decisions. When you're a salesperson, typically (like most recruiters are!) you are usually the easiest to sell to. If I walk into a car dealership, I'm the easiest person to sell a car to. If I walk into someone flogging something, I buy it. As a type of person, we're easy people to sell to, and that means we can get talked into working with the wrong people quite easily. I think we enjoy the art and respect when someone is selling to us, and there is something emotional in there for us. That isn't always an asset.

When you start your business, you will want to get the right people, but you may make some mistakes. I definitely did, and I put my hands up to that. You might take the wrong people on because you believe that everyone is like you. That is a mistake! People may look and sound the part, but make sure that you look underneath the surface for a while before committing to that person.

If you do recognise that you have the wrong person, they need to fail and fail fast. Within the first three months in recruitment, you can see if that person's going to be long-term or not. Some people say you've got to wait at least six months or at least a year. But, in my opinion, you can see the attitude, work ethic, commitment and relationship-building potential within a person in the first three months. If you do take on the wrong person, don't hold back. Wipe your mouth and move on.

As a business owner, be passionate about what you want to do, believe in the good in people but remember that *not everyone is like you*! You're going to fall down the rabbit hole if it's not working. So, get back up again, and don't let it stop you from moving forward.

Don't stand still

Standing still is the fastest way of going backwards.

When we talk about growth, there are plenty of ways to innovate. That, or you can just stand still and do nothing. If you stand still, in effect you're going backwards. You must continue to evolve, keep breaking boundaries, hit different milestones, all to make sure that you're going in the right direction. It will help if you put in clear measuring devices to see where the growth is coming from.

Then, you can channel your and your team's energy to do different things. But standing still and thinking, "We're just going to do what we have always done" means that you're always going to go backwards.

Perspective

Growth, in our industry, could mean having five people billing a total of £1m. If it goes from nothing to £1m, that's clearly huge growth. But that same figure could be reached in a completely different way. It could be that you have taken on a hundred people that each pull in billings of £10,000, which from zero, is also huge growth.

People look at growth and think that you've got to have loads of staff and a nice premises, but that's not the case. You just need to find the right sector and have the proper knowledge.

The way to achieve growth means different things to different people. For me, we're in a volume market. I've got loads of job vacancies to fill, and I need a large number of recruiters to help me harvest that crop. If you're in IT or cybersecurity, it may be that there are not as many individual invoiceable projects, but the ticket item of each one is much higher.

In my company I have looked at the following numbers to assess our scope for growth. I know that there are 52,000 people working within the property sector. There are probably 18,000 jobs in estate agency in the UK, and at least every 18 months, someone changes their job. So, looking at those 18,000 available job-filling opportunities, if we can get, as a realistic figure, 10% of those, that's something to aim for. If we decide to go for that, I then think, "How many recruiters do we need to achieve X number of placements per month to gain that revenue?" It's a basic numbers formula, which says we need X amount of recruiters that allow us to service Y amount of recruitment placements, to give us the pound note revenue we need at the end.

That's my pattern, but you might only need five people if you were in a different sector. For example, for the UK in cybersecurity, the average fee per project is £50K rather than mine at £3K. So, it's all about gearing up for the growth you need and not necessarily the size of the prize. Growth comes in all shapes and sizes.

Your core

When you're growing your business, you'll constantly be thinking about moving into different markets and different sectors. Certainly, explore them to earn additional revenue, but don't lose sight of your core. Our market is property, and naturally, in the property transaction cycle, we get new homebuying opportunities, particularly where people are first-time buyers. Most people who own property or need a mortgage require financial advice. Therefore, an add-on for us to explore is recruitment in the financial services sector linked to property purchase ie people such as mortgage brokers. Looking wider still, property obviously requires construction, so here is another whole recruitment sector allied to our core that we can explore: finding and placing people in every aspect of construction, from surveyors to bricklayers.

While growing your core business, you could potentially look outside and at other things that fall within your business's transactions. From the eyes of an estate agency, there are sales, lettings, and financial advisors in the back of the office. All the things that are sold to make them better estate agents, we can supply them. We've got into these little niches around our core. One, because we've got a name, two, because we understand the industry. Niches around your core can be much easier to focus upon than going into a whole new sector and game.

Look closer to home because you might be able to find some gold there.

It's imperative, however, to concentrate on your core. These other branches need to be secondary, additional, revenue streams. Don't focus on them as much as the core because if you do, you're just robbing Pete to pay Paul, and you're not going forward. Trust me, you'll simply be putting fires out all the time and become a busy fool rather than making more money.

Restructure around the core

When you grow a business, you grow organically, which we're trying to do now. We recruit our own people, we train them, we upskill them, and off we go. It's successful when it works, and it's been proven, in most industries, to work for decades. But you get to a point in business where you need to understand where you're going. For me, that lightbulb moment came after the pandemic when we decided we needed to restructure our plan for Rayner Personnel. We commissioned a valuation of the business and what came out of that was, "Josh, you've got a great business, but if you want to sell it for maximum value, you need to have add a temporary staffing service as part of your recruitment offering. And then you need to build this up to be 40% of your overall revenue."

Currently our assessment is that Rayner Personnel is worth three times our EBITDA (Earnings Before Interest, Taxes, Depreciation, and Amortisation). However, if we move into, as recommended, 40% of the business being dedicated to the temp sector, then it could be worth ten times EBITDA, which is a massive step up in numbers – a move from £1.5 million to £10 million.

I'm not an expert in the temp market; I've never offered temps before and have only ever made permanent placements, so currently I don't know the employment law implications and all the attendant red tape, so I would need to buy that expertise in. So, in short, sure, I could potentially build a temp business, but it might take me forever! And as I'm not going to be around forever, and I don't want to be around forever, I'd rather focus on my current area of expertise!

All that was my immediate reaction, as my instinct has been to stick to our core market. On reflection though, as you will see later with our current three-year plan, I have now come to accept that the temp market is a key part of recruitment, and of course, we are a recruitment business. So, we are pulling in the relevant expertise and off we go in pursuit of £10 million! Particularly as this is still compatible with our end goal and our Why.

Remember to keep your focus on the end goal. It's okay to pivot and explore, but always keep your WHY at the heart of everything you do.

Takeaways

- Being wedded to growth is the key to the success of the business

- If you're going to embark on setting up a business, you must give it your all

- Be wedded to your own plan and growth instead of jumping on someone else's bandwagon

- You should work with people that have bought into your vision

- As a business owner, be passionate about what you want to do, believe in the good in people but remember that not everyone is like you!

- Standing still is the fastest way of going backwards

- Niches around your core can be much easier to focus on than going to a whole new sector and game

CHAPTER SIX

Scaling Up

Scaling up, in its bare bones, is taking your business from a lifestyle business to a high-value, high-performance business that turns over a high level of revenue. Scaling up takes your business from a one-man-band to a big business where you can scale into different sectors. You can take on extra people and generate more cash. The scaling phases will usually begin with a lifestyle business, then move up to being an SME and then, at the pinnacle, an enterprise business. You must put in place different steps to grow your business; scaling is about putting the right things in place to get you there quicker.

When is a business in a position to start scaling up?

It begins with a plan, and then you need a pilot to make sure that the plan is accurate and can be tested within the relevant geographical area (where relevant). Clearly, for a purely online business, geography may not be a factor. And then, once you've got your first two or three people, it's about developing a new plan to scale that up into something far bigger. As I have mentioned before, most people don't move above ten members of staff, so, as a realistic benchmark, you need ten people plus to deal with an appropriate level of demand when you scale.

Build a strong team around you

I think many reading this book will be salespeople with a sales background and can thus, using their sales skills, generate cash. That's the essential element of your business, right, to generate cash? Right, but to run a successful business, you also need operations, finance and training. Therefore, you need to build a team around you. If you want to keep it as just your own, it will never be a big business, and you won't scale it. But when you've got people around you, you can put in place systems and processes to make sure that new staff members can replicate these easily, allowing for a streamlined business. Building a team is understanding your strengths and knowing your weaknesses and overcoming them with more heads.

At the beginning of my business days, I found it extremely challenging to be the recruiter, the marketing director and the financial controller, all at the same time. I'd be building relationships with customers, and the next minute ringing them asking them to pay their invoice.

My first two senior recruits are amazing women whom I call my 'Rayner's Angels'. One of them looks after my money and the other looks after my brand – the two most important factors in my business. They are two senior position females, both passionate people who care, can multitask, and don't mind saying "No". For me, that is an ideal combination of skills. What I can't stand in business are 'yes' people. You hire people for their experience, their expertise, but also to help you. If they are 'yes' people and simply do what you tell them to do all the time, you wonder if you could have perhaps just done it yourself.

The first person I brought on was a head of finance. I'm crap at finance – I spend more than I've got! I need someone to keep me on the straight and narrow to make sure my cashflow is in order every week, every month and on a quarterly basis, and also help me to propel my annual income. She held my feet to the fire regarding not overspending, taking money out of business, and spending money on stuff that we didn't need at that time. The good old saying 'cash is king' is bang on, so that is why I chose finance as the area for my first recruit. She had complete control of the business bank account. She could have cleaned the account out at any given time, disappeared to Spain, and never been seen again, and I wouldn't have had a leg to stand on. A massive factor for me is trust, but you've got to earn trust, and so you've got to take a punt when you hire somebody. You then work with that individual to make sure they are loyal, trustworthy and do things in the right way. Everyone makes mistakes, but as long as they can learn from mistakes, there are no problems.

My second recruit was a marketing and branding person. She helped in scaling up the brand. We carved out a great niche with the brand and our marketing efforts to penetrate our specialist market. I love marketing, but I'm no social media god. I haven't got the time or the patience to do snazzy marketing plans and implement them. So, bringing somebody into trademark the Rayner Personnel logo was vital, as I didn't know that other people could otherwise take it as their own. The marketing person helped me understand all the terms and conditions and systems and procedures. She is an all-rounder marketing guru.

On the up and up

Finance and marketing were the first two key functions I brought on to build up my brand and help me generate, and not drain, cash. They are two vital parts to my business. After that, I wondered how I could scale further. At the time, it was a franchise business, and I needed somebody who understood all the detail and was heavily operations focused. Then they can go and see the lawyers, draft up the franchise agreements and compile the operations manuals. I also needed someone to design systems and processes to support the franchisees on a day-to-day basis. All of that took a lot of detail and time, and I didn't have that – I was the visionary. So, having an operations person as my third wheel made sense. That person also acts as a great sounding board, and he always says to me, "Fast bullet, slow trigger." It grounds me and makes sure that I am doing things correctly, slowing down and keeping an eye on the detail.

Next, I realised that I needed to invest in a management team, who I previewed to you earlier. This was when I truly stepped up. I'm not a good manager of people – I've got no patience. I show you something twice and then I say, "You're just not getting it!"

I needed a leader, and that's why I brought in Russell Jervis, a great guy who inspires, energises, motivates and influences salespeople to get results. Russell is 'MD of Estate Agency', and he runs my estate agency division. I've got another guy called Jason Bushby who runs my B2B division; and Simon King is the operations director. Rachel is head of finance and vertical, and Jo looks after the marketing and supports the training and operations. That's my senior management team, and to grow to the numbers we wanted to achieve, we needed *all* those people. We couldn't have done it if just one member of that team had been missing. They have all added huge value to the cause, and as we grow even bigger, we're going to need to add to that great team.

Buying into the vision

Luckily, my first two recruits are still with me, and I am often asked how to keep a happy team. First, it's imperative to be open, honest and transparent in business, and secondly, they must buy into your vision. Your staff must fully understand what you're trying to achieve as a team and a business. You also need to be understanding; for example, Rachel has got two younger boys, so I am flexible with that in terms of the hours she is in the office. If your staff are adding value and yet you are not looking after them financially, offering time off work or flexible hours – whatever it may be – they will leave. If you have people whom you trust, for the sake of a few thousand pounds or the odd day off, I think it's essential to offer a terrific work-life balance. Respect goes both ways – I've got respect for my people, and they respect me.

But to achieve respect, you must listen and work with that individual to ensure you can do everything that's right for them. Again, if they're not suitable for the business, they need to fail and fail fast. If I do take someone on, and in three months it's not working out, I make sure that the situation is remedied. You must be ruthless, because if the early stages aren't great, then that's probably not going to change.

Takeaways

- Scaling up is taking your business from a lifestyle business to a high-value, high-performance business that turns over significant amounts of revenue

- Building a team is knowing your weaknesses and overcoming those with more, well-chosen, heads

- Everyone makes mistakes, but if your team can learn from mistakes, there are no problems

- Scaling up takes your business from a one-man-band to a big business where you can scale into different sectors

- You can take on extra people and generate more cash.

CHAPTER SEVEN

Set Long-Term Strategic Goals for Your Business

This image shows the relationship between objective, strategy and detail, and that's how I build my plan. This is taken from our recent Strategy Update presentation to our team. So, let's concentrate first on the objective. That's the top of the triangle and is the specific number you want to achieve. I have put

£10m because that is the number I want to reach in three years. Underneath that, you then have your strategy, otherwise known as your plan. Then you must ask yourself questions. For example, I now ask myself:

"For me to get to £10m how many people do I need? What sectors am I going to penetrate? How many deals will we each need to do per week, per month, per annum, to get to that £10m? And what do we need to do that is different to anybody else to make sure that we stand out as the go-to recruiter?"

Then set goals and parameters around each individual and each line manager to make sure they are achieving a mutual strategy. The management team you have brought in must have input into this plan, because they won't be as invested in executing the plan if they don't. It's OK to plan as a business owner, but if your team aren't buying into your plan and are not involved, they won't get excited as it's not theirs. So, involve them, and ask them what they would do differently. That way, they become valued and thus more valuable. It becomes their plan rather than yours, and then you can hold them accountable for their numbers. The strategy document, and the detail that supports it, breaks down the financial model into annual, quarterly, monthly, and even weekly targets so that you can monitor closely if you are hitting your numbers. That goes for anything from headcount to personal performance.

In our team, we have a weekly management call, which is about half an hour every Monday. We talk about the previous week's performance and what the plan is, going into the following week. In addition, we have a sit-down every single month as a board meeting, with the head of finance, head of marketing, the two people that head up the divisions, plus my operations director. We all sit around as a management team, and we discuss what has recently gone wrong. The key is never to be satisfied or complacent. Give praise where praise is due, for sure, but always ask questions, such as, "What do you need going forward? How are you going to smash it this month? What went right? What can we learn this month for the next month?"

We're always adding value and bouncing ideas around. We need to make sure that we are all open with one another, because we all need support. Everyone should be brought into the final vision and objective because then there will be a payday for everyone. To make sure that we get there quicker, regular meetings and being accountable to the plan is imperative. Motivation within the team is paramount to success. Especially in this model, where it can be lonely; we need to share the vision, as it affects everybody's livelihoods. We are always wondering how we are going to reward people and celebrate success.

Invest in leadership

In July 2020, I knew that I needed Russell to come in because I knew I wasn't a good manager. He was a big-ticket item, as he was then the MD of one of the largest estate agency businesses in the UK. I thought, "I need this person now. I've got to try and find a way. If it makes me take a pay cut, then so be it."

At some point, you've got to look at investing because otherwise it's the leaky bucket effect. A significant staff turnover can be highly demoralising, especially when you have worked hard to find the people, trained them up, brought them to a certain level, and *then* they leave. You feel like you're on a rollercoaster.

You must invest in making sure that people feel the love a little bit more, that they're being trained better, or that they're being encouraged more. It's great if you're putting them through courses to make them better individuals, wherever it needs to be, but you're only one person. That's why leadership expansion is critical. If you're still running a desk, fee-generating, then you can't give all five, ten, fifteen, people all your time, all the time, so it's time to bring in a leadership team.

Our culture has now changed massively from one where had franchisees to now all being licensees, and we now operate a high-performance culture. We ask people to listen to podcasts. One of our favourites is *The High-Performance Podcast*, which provides an inspiring glimpse into the lives of high-achieving, successful individuals – it's well worth checking out. We hand out books we think are valuable reads, we have top guest speakers from the recruitment sector, like Steve Guest and Greg Savage. We make proactive use of social media and have people talking about best practices. This value is to help people be better and understand that they're essential to our business and drive them forward.

It's a mindset shift to take a pay cut to bring on someone that will eventually profit the business, but that's exactly what I did when I brought in Russell. But I think that's probably why so many people don't scale up because they don't want to take what feels like a drastic step. When you start earning good money, you have a certain lifestyle and, as the saying goes, 'the more money you earn, the more money you spend, the more money you want.' I think that's a common way of life. It's hard at any stage to say, "You know what, I've got to cut back, get rid of Sky Sports for a while and lose one of the cars – I'm going to have to make some lifestyle changes."

So, instead, you backtrack at the thought of this and try to justify leaving things as they are: "No, it's fine, I can push this business forward all by myself and keep all the benefits." But then the penny finally drops, that you cannot scale up alone.

Investing in the right leadership team to take the responsibilities away from your shortcomings is critical. If you get somebody brilliant in their field, they will transform your business. That's happened for me by bringing in Russell; our culture has changed positively because of him.

It's hard to change your lifestyle and take a pay cut. I get it – no one wants to do it. But for the sake of six to nine months of sacrifice, you've now got a business that is trucking along even better. It's short-term pain for long-term gain.

Takeaways

- Motivation within the team is paramount to success

- Always look at how you can reward people and celebrate success

- You cannot scale up alone

- Invest in leadership

- Take sacrifices for longer term gains

CHAPTER EIGHT

Trimming the Fat

When you are running an SME business, you might have some basics regarding tech, such as a phone and a simple CRM system, but when you scale, you need to invest in tech that will enable you to grow in an efficient way. However, you mustn't go overboard. Some things can be expensive if they're bespoke, so looking at your overall cost per month and per head is key to ensuring that you're not overspending. Working with Simon has been a godsend for me because he's really into the detail of the contract. Every time we sign up for something, it goes through him, who then critiques the agreement inside and out. I mentioned before that I love to be sold to, but he makes sure we're not signing something that isn't going to work for us and makes sure we're running as lean as possible. He shows me that we don't need excessive tech and services.

One door closes

We are currently in the process of letting go of our head office in Bishop's Stortford because we don't need it anymore – it was a vanity item. It worked at the time, but we're now a different business. I didn't want to get rid of it, but we are now at a stage where we just need a service address in London. This will be far more efficient and won't cost £5,000 a month. We will probably find a space with a rooftop bar and a meeting room, and I'll go in there twice a week and get the team down there once or twice a week. On top of that, we can have a team-building monthly get-together now that we no longer have the need for everybody being in one room banging out the phones all day long.

It's a totally different culture now that's it's a work-from-home opportunity. We don't need to be in the office anymore, but I have kept the office a little too long for the sake of vanity and self-pride. My name is above the door and that felt good, plus it's a lovely place to work, and it also represents a massive step-up from where we were before. Currently, most of our franchisees are reasonably local to the Bishop's Stortford office, so before the pandemic, the office was packed at all times. But all that has changed due to the pandemic, and the atmosphere has been lost. Yesterday, for example, there were four of us in a 25-man office. It's not the same anymore. I have come to accept this fact, and I am now looking at the positives from leaving the office, rather than the negatives of letting it go. Look at your business and see if there are vanity items that you can let go of. As with us, the massive change in working patterns brought on so suddenly by the pandemic may just be the catalyst you need to make that move.

Be flexible with your offer

Our business is the permanent recruitment business, and thus we charge a fee once a person starts their new employment. That's the way our industry has always operated. However, we have started to look at offering alternative, more flexible fee structures: paying that fee over three or even six months; or pay a small amount every month for the lifetime that the candidate is in the job. This is a way of creating USPs and winning more business without needing to diversify into a different sector. Simply by changing the way you charge, you can find ways to stand out from your competitors and make you more attractive.

However, after you have looked at developing USPs within your sector, then of course it makes sense to look at diversifying into other revenue streams as well. For example, I knew that we had many suppliers, outside of the property sector, coming to us saying, "Josh, can you help us find development managers and sales account managers?"

I knew that their recruitment structure was different to an estate agency and that they needed a different recruitment service to that required by a typical independent estate agency. So, we scaled, diversified and created our own division of B2B.

After my experience with my first business, when I found myself 85% reliant on one client, I now try to make sure that I don't just have one big account. If you put all your eggs in one basket, you become very vulnerable. In recession times, pandemics, and the sudden impact of mergers and acquisitions, you could be swallowed up tomorrow and have nothing. Similarly, you don't want all your money in one bank account. Have some savings accounts, and other business bank accounts. If you have your money all in one place, you limit your growth.

80/20 people rule

Think about the 80/20 rule, as it can be applied to the profile of your people. You have probably got 80% of the people in the business who are steady eddies or plodders, with 20% who are superstars. Not everyone can be a superstar, and in fact you don't want 80% superstars because they can drive you crazy! Sure, they make you lots of money, but you need most people to be level-headed and consistent.

Some people naturally 'get it' quicker and better than others. There's nothing wrong with having those people who just solidly put in two deals a month, every month. By contrast, a superstar might go up and down like the rollercoaster each month. It might be ten deals one month, and zero next month, twelve the next month, and then zero, zero, zero. Then they have a midlife crisis and then they leave! (Do I sound scarred? That's because these 'superstars' have passed through our doors!) Whereas 'John' has been doing two deals every month for the last four years and gets excellent customer feedback. It's great to have 20% superstars, if your blood pressure can take it, if only to inspire and excite the rest of the team, but you also need 80% 'Johns'.

Get lean without becoming mean

Every entrepreneur needs to be flexible enough to react to changes, but it's almost impossible without long-term goals and a clear vision to work towards. It's essential to be honest about where your business is currently. You may be getting away with inefficient things right now, but if your systems are unproductive, once you scale up, this can become extremely costly. So, it's crucial to fix any inefficiencies *before* scaling. If you need to restructure the business to make it leaner, it may require cost-cutting, which isn't the most straightforward process, but is necessary in the long run.

Trimming the fat is looking at what is no longer serving you, ridding the business of those things, and either upgrading or letting go. Always look at how you can progress and what might be standing in the way of that progression.

It's essential to be transparent with your team. For example, you may need to be honest if you have taken an enormous hit during the pandemic, and you will need to let go of a few people. These are not the easiest of conversations to be had, but again, if you're honest and know you can't afford that person, then being straight and upfront with people is the best policy. Your team are people with real lives. If they've been with you for 25 years, and if you now can't afford them, or you know that you're going to come into a bit of a bad patch, it's better to give people more notice so they can find something else in the future. It's better for them. So, if things change, and you need to become leaner, then do it swiftly, but equally, if you are in a good space, you need to scale up and scale quickly.

You've got to trim the fat, but if you go through to the bone, you're dead anyway. I had to make many decisions during the pandemic on whether to lose some or all my senior management team. It turned out to not be a difficult decision, as I was confident that we would bounce back and I knew all along, as mentioned early, how essential each and every member of the management team is to our success. I knew if I cut to the bone, it would take me forever to find a team as solid as the one I have, so I absorbed the hit during those periods when we took hardly any money during parts of the pandemic lockdown period. I made sure they continued to be paid; it made so much sense to keep my dream team around me for when we bounced back. My investment has proved to be correct: we've come back out of it, and it's all going exceptionally well, but now that we are busy again, we could not have picked things back up as efficiently and effectively as we have without my dream team still fully in place. So, be lean, but if you go too lean and cut to the bone, you may end up killing your business.

It's a delicate balance, so make swift decisions, but make sure they are intelligent decisions.

Takeaways

- Look at your business and see if there are vanity items that you can let go of

- Diversify your offering

- If you put all your eggs in one basket, you become very vulnerable

- If you have your money all in one place, you limit your growth

- Trimming the fat is looking at what is no longer serving you, ridding the business of those things, and either upgrading or letting go

- Always look at how you can progress and what might be standing in the way of that progression

CHAPTER NINE

The Power of a Mentor

If you look at an Olympic athlete or look at any football star, they've all got a framework to work towards, and a mentor or a coach to keep them accountable. This is fundamental to their success. Such a framework has been trodden before and has thus becomes a blueprint of how to do things properly in the future.

In the early days of being a business owner, I knew you could succeed by putting in loads of hard work and a lot of guesswork. Guesswork is your attempts at research and understanding the market, but also involves a lot of fumbling around in the dark. It's a deep dive into the sector only wearing a pair of tights over your head. In our sector, it was all about finding ways to understand candidates and our recruiting clients' needs and understanding how, in meeting these, we could be different to anybody else. Part of that was looking at how best to harness relevant technology, but also how to move away from basic headhunting and become more of a proactive recruiter.

What I learned, in the long run, is that it all comes down to the framework. If you put suitable systems and processes in place, then you create a blueprint for success. That, coupled with sheer hard work and you will get you there quicker.

I can offer a blueprint that if you follow, will help you to be successful.

This is linked to my Why, which is wanting to help people have great lives in recruitment and to do so I have put together a training programme and mentoring service unlike any other in our industry. This has taken me fifteen years to create, and someone who has studied it has told me that it will take our competitors at least 10 years to even try to attempt to catch us up with this type of training support.

I mention that as an example, to help you to create your own blueprint for success – think about your vision for your business and for your sector, and then create your own version of something that will transform your industry and be so far ahead of your competitors. It may be the equivalent of our training programme initiative, it may be something completely different, but start working on it NOW to build that decade-long lead on the rest of the market.

When you set up your own business, there is a lot of hard work, but there's a lot of guesswork like:

"How do I set things up properly?"

"How do I win clients?"

"How do I make my business stand out?"

"What is my USP, and how am I going to be different?"

There are many unknowns if you're new into the business world and fresh into a sector. And so, you are constantly looking around to see what other people are up to and doing your research. It's a lot of guesswork, and that's normal – no one really knows where to go when you first set up. Then it begins to form into a framework; say you're looking to buy a franchise, they have a framework and a blueprint already made. Another way to help you build a solid structure to your business is to find a mentor that can give you the framework and has trodden the path and is well versed in where the business should go and the pitfalls you're going to come across. A mentor can help you set out a blueprint for what you will do in years one, two and three and make sure that you're on the right path to success.

A framework is critical in both sport and business, and having a mentor is one of the most significant factors in building that framework. A mentor can give you a good insight into where you're heading and how to avoid falling between the cracks. Setting up any new business is a rollercoaster, with huge ups and downs. You can flat line, you can lose revenue, or you can go through the roof. A mentor can keep you grounded and help you to see the obstacles.

It helps that they are not in the business. You become tunnel-visioned when you are your own boss. As your own boss, it's common to decide on a plan and be quite stubborn that you are sticking to it, but people who have an outside view can often see things that will happen before you see them. With a great mentor, that's usually because they've seen these obstacles before. A mentor is vital because you're buying expertise and experience which will help you in the long-term. You're investing in yourself by having a mentor, and the right fit will bring you many positive benefits.

How to identify a suitable mentor

I have had three significant mentors, and they are all from different walks of life. As I mentioned, I went to an all-boys school. It was an academically focused school, and I wasn't very academic. However, my head of sixth form, Mark Barrow, was a great mentor to me. He always looked sharp, and he was pretty strict. I was going through a stage of playing truant of school and generally being a rebel, and he brought me into his office by my ear. He made me stand at his desk.

"Josh, there are two paths for you. You can continue playing the wild-child card, or you can go on to be extremely successful. So, you decide what you want. But if you decide that it is success instead of the wild-child route, I want to sit you down and I will coach you to be successful."

I listened, and a deep heat of resonance sank into me.

"I want success," I said.

"Okay, so I want you to concentrate on your rugby, but also your studies, okay?"

"Okay!" I said.

He gave me a task.

"I want you to print off a list of the things that inspire you and stick it on your bathroom mirror. Think about the things that you want in life!"

As a young kid, I dreamed that when I grew up, I would have fast cars and nice suits. Mr Barrow wore a designer suit every day and clearly had a bit of money, not just from teaching. That inspired me.

"So, as I say, print off a list of all the things that inspire you, and stick them up in your bathroom. Every morning and every night, when you clean your teeth, you will go to bed with those images in your mind. You can then visualise where you're trying to get to, and you will get there faster."

That advice has stuck in my mind the whole way through my life. Thank you, Mark Barrow!

The next great mentor was John Sims, who was my first ever recruitment boss. I had known him since the age of 15. I did some silver service and waiting and bar work while I was at school, and after a short spell in estate agency, I joined him. That was my first recruitment job. John guided me when I needed some help regarding winning clients, winning candidates, and if anything happened with people not paying, he helped me handle those situations. He taught me many techniques and how to structure a recruitment business. Observing him showed me how to manage and motivate teams, and he taught me about big-picture thinking.

He was always asking me about my aspirations. He was constantly breaking me down and building me up again, asking me what was important to me and what I needed to do to be different. I can't overstate how much he helped me.

In recent years, my latest mentor, Sanjay, has been great to me. He's got a wealth of property expertise and came into property at the age of 38, so reasonably late. He has a massive property portfolio, has built a significant property business, and he's an investor and a developer. He's been instrumental in the growth of Rayner Personnel.

I asked him to come into my business 'undercover' to look inside, and he gave me some great insights and facts. One of the reasons that we pivoted from a franchise to a license was because of him. It is, of course, painful when you are told that areas aren't working, but it pays to listen. He showed me where my previous business model wasn't working and has been a fantastic third party to give me objective advice on which choices to make.

If you take on a mentor, you must trust that person implicitly. If you think they're talking rubbish, then clearly, you're not going to want to go their way – don't waste your time on a mentor that doesn't inspire you or light a fire within you.

The mentors I have mentioned were, of course, people that singled me out and mentored me personally. We all encounter potential mentors throughout our lives, but of course, as we get older, we don't have as many opportunities for people to guide us.

One route is that you can pay for a mentor, depending on a) who you want, b) how much you want to pay. Sadly, within the UK, having a mentor or a coach is often frowned upon, as many people see it as a sign of weakness. We are told to keep our stiff upper lip. Whereas in America, it's just a must to have a coach or a mentor. I think this is a culture and mindset that should shift.

If you are looking for a mentor, look for somebody that has been where you are looking to go, and somebody who has been highly successful in your arena. You can piggyback on the back of their success, understanding how they went about their business and how they were successful. Learn how to replicate that success. I know that things change, like technology and social media, but the basic principles of success don't change.

How to engage a potential mentor

You must identify where you want to go and who your 'hero' is. Then you can contact that person and say something along the lines of, "I've been following you on social media, I've been to your conferences, I've read your book, and I'm keen to borrow 45 minutes of your precious time."

Of course, try not to sound too creepy! Worded well, it should sound flattering. You don't get it if you don't ask. If they agree, you can work on building a relationship with them.

Of course, it's not entirely easy to find the right mentor immediately, either due to financial reasons or because you haven't found the right fit. If you're at that stage in your journey while reading this book, you may be about to embark on a journey to become your own boss, in recruitment or whatever sector you operate in. Maybe you've been in the business a while, or perhaps you are straight out of university, school or another industry.

The messy middle

So, if you're reading this book, hopefully, you've got to the dream stage, which is, "I really want to set up a successful company". The second phase is, "I need to have some money behind me, and then I've got to make that leap."

Whether you follow my blueprint or not, I guarantee that after about three to six months, or maybe over a year, you will hit the 'messy middle'. The messy middle is where things don't go to plan. You might have some success, but you might have some failure. It all becomes a little bit messy, and you reach a decision moment: fight or flight? Many people at that stage are not strong enough, or their vision isn't powerful enough, and they say, "Well, I gave it a go but now I'm going to get back to what I know!" So, they choose flight.

But if you do stand and fight, and bang the brick walls down and keep going, and acquire a fantastic mentor, *then* you hit the climb stage, which is the scaling stage, which we spoke about in the previous chapter.

Arrival

If you remain in fight mode, you will eventually hit 'arrival'. Arrival is achieving your KPIs regularly, your brand is out there and blossoming, and you've got the right people in the business.

It is now you can contemplate scaling. This is the exciting time where you're building a business, you've got your blueprint, your vision, and you've got the right team around you.

Josh Rayner

Arrival is building a solid business that hits the revenue numbers you want. That could be anything from X amount of turnover to how many heads you want in your business. Whatever milestones you set, the framework can then be moulded around the individual and their business. Some people desire to run a £25 million business. Some people want to run a £100,000 business; it depends on the appetite of the individual. Arrival, however, is arriving at the goal that you set yourself. You can put that vision into a planning session to decide where and when you want to reach that goal. Mine, for example, is within three years to arrive at a £10 million business. That might be made up of smaller goals along the way, and you can make mini arrivals at each milestone. The main 'arrival' is the end goal.

How a mentor can bring you to the arrival stage

Using a mentor is a wonderful way to be guided, like satellite navigation, until you arrive at your destination. They will go through each of the milestones with you but remember that a mentor isn't going to do the work for you. They will want to see you do it and be successful on your own. Most mentors have been there, done that, and got the t-shirt. If they're going to run your business, they could efficiently run your business, but that's not the point of them. The point is to hold you true to your vision as an accountability partner. Just as you would have a PT in the gym that makes sure that you hit that weight loss every week and your milestones each month, a mentor will make sure you're doing something every day to work towards your goal.

Giving back – my journey as a mentor

I have recently embarked on being a mentor myself, as I wanted to give something back to the industry. I started with a junior lettings negotiator in Manchester who worked for an estate agency business and was having an issue selling a particular product. We had weekly sessions and I fully invested in him and coached him through that whole process. It was rewarding, and I believe that I got as much from it as he did. I'm now mentoring another guy who has just embarked on building a recruitment company. It started generating revenue, but he wasn't compliant, and he could have been shut down at any time. I've now made sure that he *is* compliant. We have a strict regime where we have a call every week, and he's putting best practices, systems and processes into his business which will allow him to have a successful business rather than just a lifestyle business. So again, it is proving to be incredibly fulfilling.

Becoming a mentor has been challenging, but a great learning curve. I haven't been a mentor before, so I have been looking back at my failures and how I learned the hard way and used them to help my mentees avoid my mistakes. Much like the process for this book in fact! It keeps me on my toes, true to my beliefs and reminds me what I'm doing. I think adding value in this way makes you a better person and comes back to the serving culture again. You want to see people succeed and build a business bigger than your own. I want people to be better than me, and that's always been my philosophy. If you hire somebody, you should hire them because you think they're better at the job than you.

I am currently working on an online course with the option of mentoring at the end. I really would like to help more entrepreneurs be successful. Adding value and helping other people is my Why and my motivator. The online course is designed to help people to start their own business, so they don't fall into the pitfalls that I did. I believe that a successful recruitment business is built on the three 'R's: Relationships, Reputation and Recommendation. My new online course is titled *10 Steps to Success* and in it I show people how to achieve success by realising their vision. Step by step, it helps business owners to establish their own reputable brand and gives them the tools needed to build their own successful business, in the recruitment sector or elsewhere.

Takeaways

- You need to define your core values for your business

- Having a mentor is one of the most significant factors in building a successful business framework

- You become tunnel-visioned when you're your own boss

- Print off a list of the things that inspire you and stick them up in your bathroom

- Don't waste your time on a mentor that doesn't inspire you or light a fire within you

- If you take on a mentor, you must trust that person implicitly

- You can piggyback onto their success, understanding how they went about their business and how they were successful

- If you remain in fight mode, you will eventually hit 'arrival'

- Remember there are three ways to success; guess work, hard work or framework

CHAPTER TEN

Process Sets You Free

'Success is addictive but remember, there are no shortcuts on any road you're travelling, so trust and follow the process every time and you will succeed.'

Josh Rayner

I come from a serving mindset. My **Why** is to help people and to add value to people in my industry. Thus, I would like to share how processes have saved me time, stress and money. Every area of our business is process-driven, and it saves us so much time and money.

Process sets you free, especially in recruitment. You must organise your time to maximise your return. Over the years, we have found the systems and processes to build into our business to make it far easier for things to happen and give the customer a better service. Routine and process will set you free, and then you can be your own entrepreneur. If you don't have a routine and you think, "You know what, today I'm going to ring a hundred random people and try and get this job filled," it doesn't work, and you become a busy fool rather than adding value.

When you set up your business, be it in recruitment or elsewhere, you need to have processes for every division of your business. Once you have a process in situ, the more successful you'll be.

I'm all about process, diary management, and solutions. We've broken down everything from 8 am through to 6 pm in the company, including what a consultant should be doing every hour. That is unique to our industry and ensures we know when people are in team meetings and when they're out and about. It's about understanding what a typical candidate and client diary looks like and then mapping our consultants' diaries around this to make sure they can speak to people at the correct times of the day. In the recruitment industry, it's always candidate-led and not job-led. It's all about finding the right candidate for the job. And in any sector, processes should be client-led in what they are aiming to achieve.

We spend three days of the week specifically looking for new candidates, and the other two days are devoted to client retention and picking up new jobs. You need 50/50 in most processes, but it makes sense that we need more candidates than we do assignments. So, we spend 80% of the week doing the candidate side of things and 20% clients. You must be prospecting every day and be different and innovative in your approach to build relationships that last.

Going to market with a new role – our process

How we go to market with a new job vacancy is a process that has been newly defined over the last year:

1)   We speak to a client and initially agree to the terms of business.
2)   We then make a discovery call to understand the job as much as they do, so you are as passionate as they are.
3)   Then we put it into our system, which will make posts out to the broader market and across social media.
4)   Now we go out and find candidates for that role.
5)   We use our database views, other job board databases, manage applications, profile people, and then we look at headhunting off-market talent. That means we go out there and do mystery shopping so that we've got intelligence regarding league tables etc., that gives us an idea of market share.

6) Then we put together a shortlist and review that with the client.

7) We book in the interviews.

That's pretty much how our process works from start to finish.

How do I begin putting processes in place?

This of course depends on your sector, but you can take our framework and implement a version of it in your industry. I've got champions in my business that do that. For example, my finance lady wants to have things done a particular way, so she has created the process for the accounting side of things. It's tried and tested. We have tweaked it until we have got it right. She has owned that process, and that has worked out brilliantly. If someone owns the process correctly, they will believe in it more and be more likely to follow it. The candidate journey process has come from me, and then my operations guys have put it into action. Our people in sales have worked up a detailed sales process. It's essential to find somebody that knows and understands what works and then documents that into a process.

It has taken me four years to get to this point of deep process in the business. But it doesn't have to take that long. I promise, the faster you put in the process, the quicker your success will be.

Previously there had not been enough detailed process in the recruitment space, a general weakness in our industry. And so, we needed to start with the end in mind. It's all about the customer – whether it's the candidate or the client, you must have the customer in focus. That's what we're doing it for. Then build systems and processes behind that focus to ensure the candidate has at least X-amount of touchpoints throughout the whole process. This reasoning is to ensure they're engaged and understand what's going on. You don't just say, thanks for your CV and never speak to them again. A simple thing, but it has helped us by recording how many times we have talked to each candidate during the process and document how we have presented feedback from clients etc.

So, I think all new business owners need to think about process early doors. We now have a blueprint that we can share with you, if relevant, to map into your business.

Of course, you can work without processes and wing it for a while, but it will then stubbornly remain a lifestyle business. You will never leverage what you could potentially have because if you haven't got these systems and processes in there, you will always fall behind.

As I have mentioned many times in this book, for a long time, I was a busy fool, a Jack of all trades and a master of none, spinning so many plates that I didn't concentrate on the critical stuff. It might be that you've got a particular project that pays the right money, but then another assignment comes in, or another client comes on board, or you've got to chase a client for some cash because you haven't got a process in place. Without processes in place, setting clear priorities and dividing up tasks to the most appropriate people, all this becomes just firefighting, and it wastes a lot of time. If you have a process in play, you can manage your whole day in your diary, and it's easier to get more done, and you'll be much more effective.

Of course, people see the word process, and they think that it's not for them. But, having worked in both ways, I can promise you that you save a lot of time and witness a lot more success with processes in place.

Without process, you end up stuck in a lifestyle business, and so are unlikely reach higher levels of success. If you want to scale a business and have something saleable, you must remember that people are not buying *you*; they're buying the business, and the value of the business without any systems and processes is pretty much zero. And if you were going to build a business based on maverick behaviour, it probably isn't worth anything. The processes and the systems are the foundations of the business.

Ask yourself, "If I walked away from this business today, would it still run?"

If the answer is no, you need to put processes in place. If those processes are not in place, the business won't have a lot of allure. There might be some business coming in, but there are documents all over the place, and, depending on your sector, it may well not even be industry compliant.

Routine allows you to get some time back. For example, if you've got a process for collecting cash, it just hits your account. Then you can concentrate on other, more creative things.

Examples of processes

As I have emphasised throughout this chapter, we have processes in place right across every aspect of our business. Here, using some examples from our recruitment business, are how some useful processes can be built up, ensuring a smooth path through the entire sales cycle.

Registering & qualifying candidates

As soon as we have found a candidate, we need to register them, and thus ask them all the right questions to understand the motivations of the person looking for a job. It's not always about salary. This is usually a 45-minute conversation to understand where they are, their family requirements, their location requirements, and would they work weekends. What are the main drivers for them looking for a move? Once we understand that, and we've got their CV, it's about critiquing that CV. We then do a video with that individual of five minutes long and get a good understanding of their attitudes regarding working culture.

Are they a high performance or competitive kind of person, or are they more laid back? Perhaps they are more systems and process led, or perhaps, more back-office. It's essential that we get a good understanding of that. Then I would take that candidate to market. I would initially go out to the clients I know are looking for candidates with a particular background. If not, I would ask if I could speculatively introduce the candidate to people that are not clients of mine. It's about working in partnership with that candidate and marketing that candidate effectively and professionally. In our business, we want our consultants to make at least four placements a month.

So, if we've got four candidates on three interviews every single week, we know one of them will be placed. This is easy for our consultants to understand. "I know that I've got to have four people out for interviews, which means arranging 12 interviews, and two of them are going to be job offered. One will take the job and happy days!" It's following a process so that the consultant can earn revenue and that the candidate and the client are getting the service they require.

CRM for candidates

Every relevant person in our business has access to the CRM that tracks the candidates. We have tweaked our CRM to make it work for us. The CRM takes a candidate on a bit of a journey. So, when we enter their information, it tells the candidate what to do regarding company research, makes sure they dress appropriately, arrive on time etc. We also pick up the phone for that vital human interaction and relationship with that individual, but the CRM tracks that candidate throughout the system. Once we have placed that candidate, it alerts our accounts team, who then raise an invoice. The CRM takes a candidate from day one through to placement.

CRM for clients

For clients, it's a similar process. Firstly, we need to take the brief for the job description, which is a form that we use over the phone, and it goes into the system. We put the job on the system, which then pings it out to free job boards. It creates a social media banner that the client can use on LinkedIn or other social media platforms. If you apply, we can see which platform that interested party has come from.

If we know that most people are coming from our website, we spend more money on pay-per-click. Or if Reed's, Reed.co.uk, is working for us, then we spend more money on our Reed accounts. We like to find out exactly where our candidates and clients come from and then spend more money where we need to. Our CRM is set up with all of that in mind.

Marketing and branding process

Branding is essential to me; we need to stand for something, both from a candidate and a client point of view. And we DO stand for something – in everything we do, we aim to attract the BEST talent, that talent that an employer wants to hire and the talent a recruiter wants to speak to. To do this, we need to be slick, professional, approachable and build robust relationships. So, we post out about different aspects of our business and our services on particular days. So, on Mondays, we post our jobs. Tuesdays and Thursdays, we post reviews of our service, with client reviews and candidate reviews on different days. We also publish various bits and pieces around the typical working week.

You need a process for registering for a job. You need a process for candidates, clients, and marketing. You need a process for invoicing and credit control. You need a process for management. You need a process for HR. For example, if you have 150 people working for you, you need a process regarding employees going on a holiday, being sick, or leaving. So, we have a starters and leavers process and an onboarding process.

Accepting the process

Although most salespeople hate processes and just want to crack on and pick up the phone and make some money, remember that you will only have limited success without process. Let's use a sporting analogy. Any sport: rugby, chess or tennis etc., has processes in its training which are highly specialised. So, to be an elite athlete, you must follow a specific process to become the best. The same process that the elite athletes in that sport have refined and developed. So, somebody might go into a business and think, "Oh, I know better. I just want to make some money, and I don't care about the process."

But, if that is your attitude, do you think that David Beckham just went in and started knocking a few balls around in the garden on his own and suddenly became world-renowned and rich? No, there was a clearly defined process that he undertook.

Reviewing the process

Of course, it's essential to review the process regularly. So, when there's an England rugby game, the team will sit down afterwards and rewatch the match. They will discuss what they could do to improve, why the scrum wasn't strong and what tweaks they need to make to improve. You must keep reviewing your systems and processes because things change.

So, for example, video interviewing is now the norm and is part of the process which didn't exist before Covid-19. You must constantly review your process to ensure it is market-leading, as sloppy processes affect your brand and your service.

Takeaways

- You must organise your time to maximise your return

- You must be different and innovative in your approach to build relationships that last

- The faster you put in the process, the quicker your success will arrive

- If you want to scale a business and have something that, in the end, is saleable, you must remember that people are not buying *you*; they're buying the business

- The value of the business without any systems and processes is zero

- Your business and the marketplace changes, so review your processes regularly

CHAPTER ELEVEN

The Three-Year Plan

When I first started, and when most people start, they have a plan to get going. At this time, they're typically employed, and they think they want to leave their current employer and set up a business. They want to make as much money as possible and drive nice cars. They want a lovely lifestyle and want to see their family more. That's pretty much 'the plan'. That was my plan at least, and I'm sure that of millions of people before me too. To achieve that, sitting down and adequately planning the first three years of your business is critical. You need to know where you're going, so mapping it out means you are more likely to foresee and overcome the many minor hidden obstacles that will slow you down during your journey. Some people create five-year plans, but I believe that a three-year plan is far enough ahead to have in place.

Your plan's objective

It's easier to control three years, and it's a lot easier to work with. I break it down into the plan's objective, its strategy and detail, and the vision of what I want to achieve in three years. That means a lot of digging and deep soul searching. Again, this is about remembering your Why. It is remembering what you're trying to do and why you're trying to do it. What is your objective? A business could just be a lifestyle business to give you some freedom. It could be about managing a buyout or getting to the point where you can float the business for sale. It is critical that you have worked out where you want to head so that the objective is right. My objective, for example, is that I want to make £10m in the business in the next three years.

I want my business to be worth £10m, so that it becomes sufficiently attractive for other people to want to purchase it. That's what it needs for me to be noticed as a big player and a big fish, and for buyers to be attracted to Rayner Personnel – that's my objective. To get into why that's attractive to me is that it allows me to lead the business. I can stay in the business; I might not want to sell it, especially if it becomes a big business that can do something inspiring. There is no point in building something that isn't valuable.

The strategy is to get my whole leadership team involved in the plan so they will own it too. If they don't own the plan, then it's just my ideas, and they are just doing what I have told them to do. Whereas, if they have had loads of input, which they have, they take ownership of it, which keeps them accountable.

Your plan's strategy

It helps if you have done your research. If ultimately selling the business is your plan you first need to understand your potential purchaser and what you're building because if you build a business that's not attractive to others, what's the point?

Also, during building your plan, you need access to granular detail; in our case breaking down how many heads we have, how much revenue each consultant will generate and what we need to keep putting into the business to make it work. There are lots of variables around that.

My operations manager is into the detail, which I am not great at, and that input has exponentially improved our business. If you haven't got an operations manager, a coach or a mentor can help. It's all too easy to get locked into tunnel vision, focusing just on the day-to-day job, so that you end up being unable to see outside the four walls of your business. In my case, I was locked in a room for a day by my director; no phones, no distractions, to ignore the next three days and focus instead on the next three years.

"Josh, the first thing is that the past is the past. We can't change the past; it is what it is. We now need to concentrate on the future. We've got a whole new business model, and the objective is to get this business to a £10 million valuation in three years!"

Our plan

So, we talked at length about the strategy of getting us there. The following is what our three-year plan looks like, in a nutshell. This was written down in August 2021.

2021 is about laying the foundations for 2022; we are building a bridge. We discussed how there are only four months left of the year and that moving forward was about getting the right people in our business and get them up and running quickly. Covid has showed us that we need more tech in our business to function better as a team and be able to see where people are struggling, so we can nip in and help them. But effectively, it's about getting all that ready so that when we get to January 2022, we're all systems go, ready to put a rocket up our backsides and make it happen. 2022 isn't just about hitting the plan; it's about maintaining that plan. We have decided that we need 25 people, geographically based, each netting three placements per head per month.

- 2022 is all about sustainability. We've got the plan, the people, and the team needed to make sure that people are hitting the plan. That gives us the cash to do something even more exciting in 2023.
- In 2023, we are launching a temp division in our business.
- 2024 is about keeping everything sustainable, and then we're going to float the business on the market and see what happens. There must be plenty of cash in the business so that it is seen as attractive. We want prospective buyers to not feel that they are buying a problem child; they're buying a rich EBITDA company to offset a negative one.

So that's our three-year plan. As I have said, I believe that things are moving too quickly to construct a meaningful a five-year plan.

I have learnt a lot about planning during the pandemic. We had this plan before Covid, but we lost a year, so we must bear that in mind. We also have an ageing workforce, as our senior management team are in their fifties. I think you can gain a clear kind of objective in three years, but five years seems a little bit out of reach. Three years goes pretty quick; also, when you bring in self-employed people, three years seems like 20 years to them.

Whatever your plan is, make sure it's realistic and achievable because you will become miserable constantly if you're not hitting your milestones. Being realistic in the plan helps to keep the team focused as well. Every month, we say, "Jason, you agreed on this three-year plan. In April, you said we would do X amount of revenue, and we've only done Y. What do I need to do to give you the support to hit that plan?"

Of course, achieved milestones must be celebrated. So again, it is best to work with your people to make sure they have bought into taking on accountability. I think that's the bit that I have found helpful in getting people involved in building the plan and using transparency, as everybody feels involved in its development. Everyone should feel ownership and that it's their business as well as mine. That way, they become more passionate about it, they're on it all the time, and they want it to succeed. That's what it's all about! If they're not given autonomy, they think they're just a slave to somebody else. If you don't believe in something, you're not going to work as hard as if you did. Everyone should be in the same boat, rowing in the same direction.

Whether they're a junior or the owner, everyone in the business needs to be in the boat, going in the same direction and embracing the plan. If you have somebody in there that isn't entirely on board, the boat goes off balance, and eventually, everybody sinks. If you identify that person, get rid of them quickly before that eventuality. If everybody believes in the same goal, with the same mission, you will get there much faster.

People have wings

As I have mentioned, I've undertaken some consulting recently with an estate agency business. I got involved and built a self-employed model for them. This cohort now for accounts for 50% of their revenue within just six months, and they've been running for 15 years. They're excited, but when someone leaves, they become so devastated that it knocks their confidence. This has made them rethink when they're hiring people, as it has taken a sparkle from what the business used to be like.

"Look," I said, "you have got to understand that this is not for everybody. We are in the sales business. Recruitment's the same – the life cycle of a salesperson is about 18 months. So, be realistic and remember you will get a good 18 months out of a person and then they will probably leave. Sure, you can freeze share options and offer bigger percentages, but ultimately, I don't think there's a job for life anymore. My dad has been with his employer since he was 21, and that is a job for life. But millennials and Gen X, Y and Z don't want that. They're on a journey for themselves. Some of them will want to stay, and some of them will go. That's okay; deal with it positively and wish them good luck. Just make sure in the plan you have taken this into account."

I know that in my business, each month, I need to take on a minimum of two people to make sure that I'm always servicing my customers correctly. If people put in their notice, it's okay because we are ahead of it, we've dealt with it, and we've got a plan. Remember too, that too many superstars will change your business dynamic because they start to make everyone else becomes too aggressive in their sales technique. They try too hard to smash targets every month and, without the rare skill of the superstar, become that pushy salesperson that no one wants to deal with. A different, but similarly corrosive effect can happen if you have too many plodders. Even the previous superstars then slow down, and everyone starts to feel content just plodding along, and the whole business ends up standing still and then going backwards. Remember that a balanced workforce is critical. If you get the blend right, you achieve good, steady, consistent growth rather than a disruptive rollercoaster of activity. **Consistency is key!**

Surprise!

Don't expect the best – plan for the worst. I'm
always prepared to be surprised.

You can have the best plan in the world, but you might have an unpleasant surprise if you don't plan for the worst. It's challenging to prepare for the worst, but remember that in business, cash is king. It's common to fall over yourself and think, "Wow, I've got so much more than I'm paying myself", but then you go and buy all the toys and spend the money on the tech you don't need. So always make sure you leave 60% revenue in your business and only take a maximum of 40% out. It really is important to leave 60% buffer in there. I know it's exciting when you start your own business and start seeing good money, but if you don't plan for the worst and have a financial backup plan, then you're in real big trouble if the worst happens. After all, who of us at the beginning of 2020 saw the massive disruption of the pandemic being just around the corner? Whereas if you've got some cash behind you, you'll be okay.

Again, if economic planning isn't your jam, then find somebody who can help you. In any area of your plan, make sure that you have the best brains in each area to achieve the best results.

Plan B & C

Of course, it is essential to focus on your plan, but it's also imperative to have a Plan B and a Plan C. If the marketplace changes overnight (again, think pandemic), you must have an option B and C, even if they're at the back of your mind. If the plan needs to change, and you need to pivot, you need to shift quickly. Don't overthink plans B and C, but make sure you've got a robust second and third backup.

Do you need help with your 3-year plan?

I have put together a course, titled *The 10 Steps to Success...*

A version of this course is aimed specifically at those wanting to start and run their own successful business in the industry in which I operate and have been successful, recruitment. However, as the tick list below illustrates, there is a version too which is aimed at *anyone* wanting to launch and scale a successful business, in any sector.

Topics covered included:

- Escape the 9-5 rat race and become your own boss. You set the pace.
- Launch your own company from scratch.
- Run & manage your own business from home or from anywhere in the world.
- The details: creating your terms of business. Required registrations and insurances.
- Realise your vision & the size of the prize.
- Look at the HR model, staffing, contracts & handbooks, NI & pension contributions.
- Understand the power of a brand and becoming an influencer.
- Learn how to win clients and add value to your business.
- Learn how to source the best talent.
- Choose the right systems & write the processes to set you free.
- Secure your financial freedom.
- Learn how to win the week with successful diary management & organisation.
- The simple, concise steps to follow covering all aspects of running your own business.
- The financials, how to manage your credit control, payments & refunds
- Complete the course and be armed & ready to launch your own business.

Takeaways

- Adequately planning the first three years of your business is critical

- Whatever your plan is, make sure it's realistic and achievable because you will become miserable constantly if you're not hitting your milestones

- Don't always expect the best – plan for the worst. I'm always prepared to be surprised

- In any area of your plan, make sure that you have the best brains in each area to achieve the best results

Final Thoughts

I appreciate you riding this rollercoaster with me. Remember, buckle up, do your research, meet great people, make some mistakes, and shoot for your dreams.

*Remember, rollercoasters are supposed to
be both scary and fun — so enjoy.*

I wish you every success on your ride.

Joshua Rayner